how to be

Fit & Free

HOW TO HAVE A HEALTHY, TRIM BODY WITHOUT DIETING, THROUGH THE RIGHT-WAY-OF-EATING

Rick Kasper

A Division of G/L Publications
Glendale, California, U.S.A.

Other good Regal reading:
The Best Half of Life
by Ray & Anne Ortlund
Strategy for Living,
by Edward R. Dayton
and Ted W. Engstrom

The foreign language publishing of all Regal books is under the direction of *Gospel Literature International* (GLINT), a missionary assistance organization founded in 1961 by Dr. Henrietta C. Mears. Each year *Gospel Literature International* provides financial and technical help for the adaptation, translation, and publishing of books and Bible study materials in more than 85 languages for millions of people worldwide.

For more information you are invited to write *Gospel Literature International*, Glendale, California 91204.

Second Printing, 1978
Third Printing, 1978

Published by Regal Books Division, G/L Publications
Glendale, California 91209
Printed in U.S.A.

Library of Congress Catalog Card No. 77-089398
ISBN 0-8307-0580-5

contents

preface

Much of what you read in this book is a product of my personal experiences. I have been very light, 135 pounds, and I have been very heavy, 255 pounds. I know what it feels like to *gain* a lot of weight in a short period of time—82 pounds in nine months! I know what it feels like to *lose* a lot of weight in a short period of time—64 pounds in eight weeks! I have tried many diets and suffered through programs which, if we subjected our enemies to them during wartime, would be considered violations of the Geneva Convention. I know the frustrations of not looking the way I want and not feeling the way I would like to.

Because of injuries, accidents and a fairly frail body, I wanted to be as healthy as possible. So, while many friends and associates spent years in conventional education at a college or university, I devoted my energy and time to finding out all I could about health. I went to college, but most of my time was spent in gyms, spas and health-food stores. I had opportunity to be associated with and study under several brilliant men in the field of health, including Bud Keith and Jack LaLanne. I have seen changes in physical appearances and energy levels that you would not believe.

I was learning some of the things I had started out to learn. The pieces of the health picture were fitting together, but something was still missing. After many futile attempts to complete my life, I realized I had not worked on the spiritual side. It wasn't until I met God's Son, Jesus Christ, and invited Him into my life as my personal Lord and Saviour that everything fell into place. For years I sought health at the expense of all other areas. Now Jesus Christ is balancing out my life and giving me direction where before there was none. I now have a reason for living and a reason for taking care of this marvelous body God has given me.

First Corinthians 6:19,20 tells me that my body is the temple of the Holy Spirit. Because the Holy Spirit dwells in me, and in everyone who has entered into a personal relationship with Jesus Christ, my body is a consecrated body. A fat or run-down body brings glory and honor to no one. Not to God and not to me.

Are you glorifying God with your body? God requires us to be good stewards of our time, our money and our talents. How are you doing as a steward of your body? Are you strengthening your body through good health habits or do you ignore your dusty tabernacle until it falls into disrepair?

Christian reader, we are saved by grace, not works; salvation is a gift of God (see Eph. 2:8,9). Taking care of your body obviously will not save you, only a personal relationship with Christ can do that. But how many testimonies have been negated and how many potentially powerful lives have been of no effect because the Christian neglected his human body? We demonstrate the power of Jesus Christ when we bring our bodies under submission. Our appearance testifies to the energy we have when we are not enslaved by unhealthy habits. Can the world see the vitality of God shining through us, or do our tired eyes and out-of-shape bodies make our lives and our message unattractive.

Romans 12:1 is one of my favorite verses. It presents, I think, an excellent approach to our bodies. "I beseech you therefore, brethren, by the mercies of God, that ye present your bodies a living sacrifice, holy, acceptable unto God, which is your reasonable service." When we become Christians we turn our whole being over to God. We no longer belong to ourselves, we belong to God. What kind of bodies are we presenting to God. Are they holy and acceptable?

We tell the world much about ourselves by the way we care for our bodies. "Put your best foot forward" is sound advice. But I would like to change that adage slightly, *put your best body forward*. Reach for the best body you can have and really enjoy this life. *Be Fit and Free!*

part one

What This Book Is All About

Introduction

introduction

"Fatties" and their problems of overabundance are the most popular subjects on today's bookshelves. Everywhere we look another answer for the fat question appears; another miracle diet, another clinically-tested, hospital-approved way to lose weight painlessly and without boring exercise. Evidently FAT is *not* where it's at. But can any of these "miracle diets" substantiate their claims? We find so many of them. Do any of these diets work?

How to Be Fit and Free is unlike any other book you have ever read. You will discover that the program in this book works and the results are permanent.

Someone is always concocting a new way to lose weight. Gimmicks, gadgets, wraps, special diets and shots are just a few of the mind-boggling ways to lose those ugly extra pounds. *How to Be Fit and Free* will explain why other programs are short-ranged. We will get to the root causes of overweight. We will discuss habits and the relation they have to the poundage you carry.

Unfortunately, most of us know little about our bodies and how they function. And we take small notice of our physical apparatus until it ceases to perform as we wish. Then we rush off to buy a new book on weight loss or dash to the drugstore or to some member of the professional community to purchase a product or procure some advice which will *immediately* eliminate the problem. Usually we treat the effects of the problem and never reach the cause.

Should losing weight come under the jurisdiction of the medical profession, the majority of whom spend little time in prevention of health problems and even less time in teaching nutrition? Are drugs and shots and starvation healthy ways to shed extra poundage?

I agree we need our doctors, our hospitals, our medical community and possibly even drugs at some time in our lives. I cannot believe, however, that we should totally attribute our health and well-being to doctors and drugs. No less an authority than Hippocrates, the father of medicine, observed that the physician's purpose is to help the body heal itself. He believed in using as few drugs as possible, allowing the body to perform the real job of healing.

Although the world has changed considerably since the early days of medicine, the human body is still the human body. Modern problems have arisen because of the way we live and because of the environment in which we live. Modern medicine is facing ponderous questions of immense importance. But possibly the most important, the most prevalent and the most confusing health problem we face as a country is *fat*.

11

In today's world we are programmed to accept anything that makes life easier and that helps us perform our chores quicker. We live surrounded by gadgets and gimmicks. Our household chores are made easier through modern electronic inventions. Television and radio inform us of events and achievements we would not normally be aware of. We enjoy thousands of modern aids that decrease our work load and increase our leisure time. And amid the array of mechanical marvels we encounter unbelievable gimmickry in the battle of the bulge.

Because we have been conditioned to expect results and expect them now, not in six months or a year but NOW, overweight people as a rule tend to be impatient. They fail to realize, or manage to overlook, the fact that it took a long time to establish their weight problem. Oh, they may have gained 10 or 15 pounds just in the past year, but the mechanism for adding this weight has been operating for a long time. However, there is a way the overweight person can lose fat quickly and *keep it off*, without gimmicks.

The material in this book will seem so simple and obvious that you will probably say, "I know that. It's common sense." We need to use more of our common sense, or uncommon sense, when it comes to our bodies. Let us not take a simple problem like being overweight and make it complicated. Complexity only gives us an excuse for failure and an escape when we break the diet rules we set down for ourselves.

You may argue that you are different and have not yet found the proper diet or program that best suits your body. Well, this program works on all types of people under all circumstances, if they *really want to lose weight*. The solution to your weight problem may well be a drastic about-face in your mode of living. I pray that

How to Be Fit and Free will free *you* from the security blanket of poor health habits and place you on a strong foundation of health principles which will give you the body you want with health you deserve.

I can say, without a doubt, if you follow the program explained in this book, you will *for sure* lose all your excess weight and lose it for good. This program will fit easily into whatever life-style you lead as long as you really *want* to change your shape and alter your appearance and, at the same time, improve your physical condition—*outside and inside.*

If you don't have a weight problem, that's great. You can concentrate totally on gaining better health by learning what to eat, what not to eat, and by eliminating certain unhealthy habits that rob you of some of the good things in life. Apply the principles in this book and be truly *Fit and Free!*

chapter one
Fat Is Not Where It's At

Have you ever thought that being overweight is a sickness? It is, you know. Oh, you may call it your "little problem" or laughingly refer to your "winter coat." You may even add that your whole family is a little heavy—you inherited it. Or you may say, "I need this extra weight." But regardless of the excuse, being overweight is far from being healthy. For every pound of fat your body carries, it must produce 4000 extra feet of capillaries to feed this fat. This extra effort creates a tremendous strain on your whole body but especially on your muscular system. The most important muscle being your heart. If you continue to overstrain or overwork any muscle you will prematurely wear out the muscle. Excess fat definitely overstrains your heart muscle, creating an added work load for an already very active organ.

Seventy years ago coronary cases were so rare that few medical students had the opportunity to study them. Now heart disease is one of the most common killers visiting our homes. Being overweight definitely multiplies your chances for a heart attack. But in addition to being a threat to your heart, many degenerative diseases, and regular not-so-serious infirmities, gain their foothold via the weakening power of fat. The overweight person is destined for catastrophe in one of his possessions he can't exchange, replace or always effectively repair: HIS BODY.

Your Waistline Is Your Lifeline

Besides the damaging effect excess weight has on the heart, other conditions convince us that fat should scat.

Being overweight is not very attractive. Recent women's fashions—short skirts, tight shorts, fat-fitting pants—leave little to the imagination. Men's pants used to fit snugly above the pelvic bones and caused the wearer to be more conscious of holding his waist in. They required belts that could be tightened and would pinch his stomach in a bit. Pants today are often made of polyester—they give where you give—so these stretch-type pants fit loosely and allow an already soft, sagging waistline to sag even more. Thus our middles relax and we forget to hold ourselves erect. Little wonder our bulge bulges without reproof.

Fat impedes digestion. Doctors regularly listen to complaints about stomach problems. In fact, few of us seem to be immune to some kind of digestive ailment. The more weight you carry around your middle, the more strain you place on your internal organs, especially your digestive organs. When fat collects around your middle, it cramps blood vessels that feed these important digestive organs. If circulation is impeded your stomach cannot effectively digest food. Ultimately, poor digestion means poor nutrition. You may eat all the basic foods necessary to obtain and maintain a balanced diet, but if your body cannot assimilate these foods throughout your body, you are wasting your time and money, as well as your health.

Fat around your middle is also uncomfortable. I once saw Jack LaLanne illustrate this point very graphically. He spread just one pound of white animal fat from the butcher shop around his waist. Then he commented how uncomfortable it would be to carry just a one-pound layer of fat around his waist day and night. Now imagine the discomfort of carrying an extra 20 or 30 pounds— under your skin where you can't get at it to scrape it off!

The fat habit is expensive. In this age of overspiraling food costs we are extremely conscious of the short distance the dollar travels. As you contemplate your budget, remember that being overweight is an expensive habit. It takes much more to feed a body of 200 pounds than one of 130 pounds. Because fat cells are living cells, they need to be nourished like all other cells in the body.

Excess fat increases your disease aptitude. I have not seen an extensive study on this topic, perhaps because almost all of us have a little weight problem, but I certainly believe that you increase your disease aptitude as you increase your weight. By disease aptitude I mean the condition of the body which makes it easy prey for such health problems as diabetes, coronary disease, hardening of the arteries, and other not-so-serious ailments like colds and minor infections.

An overweight body must work harder to feed what it normally should feed, plus feed the fat. This extra work seriously taxes your whole system, and a body that must work hard all the time becomes a weakened system. If your body must use the protein you eat to feed the enormous amounts of fat you are carrying, then there aren't enough nutrients to produce antibodies to fight infections and to raise the level of resistance.

An obese person normally has bad circulation. Cold hands and feet are symptoms of strain on the circulatory system, for your hands and feet are not getting the nutrients necessary for the removal of waste products. We often overlook cold hands and feet, but our body doesn't.

Some fat people use their weight problem as an emotional shield. I am not a psychiatrist, but I have discovered that many people who want to lose weight use food, especially sweet food, as a pacifier to help them cope with the frustrations of life. In this way their weight problem is an emotional shield. They hide behind it like a child hides under the covers when he is afraid. Men and women both use sweets as a crutch (alcohol should also be classified in this group since it is almost all carbohydrate) when they have been emotionally wounded, suffered a setback in occupation or recreation, or when they crave a reward for enduring a difficult task—like staying on a miserable diet! Then when the weight starts to pile back on they eat more sweets to get an emotional lift to help them cover up their self-guilt for gaining the weight.

This sweet cycle is damaging to the person involved, but it is also doing immeasurable damage to those around that one. How can a woman unreservedly return love to a man when she is disgusted with herself for being fat? She can't give what she doesn't feel.

In fact, no one can truly love another unless he feels that he is basically a good person, worthy of being loved. If he really considers himself a worthwhile individual, he recognizes that feeding his face is a selfish, draining activity; draining because he recycles back into himself the potential love as he satisfies himself by his eating habits.

Food supplies nothing but nourishment. Not love, not compassion, not satisfaction—just nourishment. Eating can be an emotional crutch that leads to self-guilt that leads back to eating as an emotional crutch. Too often we live to eat rather than eat to live.

Overweight Means Overaging

I am appalled at the number of people who are over-weight today. They form a club whose membership is swelling. However, I am less shocked at their over-weight condition than I am at their aged appearance. Women seem to age by the minute when they gain weight. Their faces get puffy and muscles, weakened by the extra flesh, sag and hang loosely. Blood vessels appear closer to the skin, eyes are baggy and their complexion looks like it belongs on someone much older.

Men are not, by any means, exempt from the effects of physical abuse and overindulgence in food. On a recent trip back East, I conducted a private survey on the physical appearance of the American male. Perhaps one man out of 50 looks as if he could do some strenuous activity if necessary. The other 49 had pot bellies, poor posture and sagging jowls.

Once upon a time a man's success was partially gauged by his weight. Only the very rich could afford to be fat. Today, sharp increases in heart problems and hardening of the arteries make fat a luxury none of us can afford. And yet we get fatter and fatter each year. While fat is definitely not pretty on the outside, it is much uglier on the inside where it crowds the internal organs and robs the body of nutrients, energy and vitality, as well as useful, productive years.

If you have been overweight for a prolonged period

you may have convinced yourself that excessive weight inevitably accompanied you at birth and that no personal effort can negate this inherited characteristic. Meanwhile you are wasting the strength of your youth and the advantages of a healthy heritage. Your body defenders, forced to work overtime, will eventually give up, setting the stage for the degenerative diseases we mentioned. Not everybody, of course, who is overweight contracts diabetes or suffers hardening of the arteries or arthritis, but many do. The coincidence is staggering.

Think also of the damage you, as a parent, may do to your offspring. Fat is not inherited, but the tendency to be fat can be. You were not born to be fat. If you are now fat it's because you were trained to be; trained by *your* parents' eating habits, the diet of your youth and the style of physical activity you have grown accustomed to. You may be supplying your own children with eating habits and addictions that will encumber them the rest of their lives. It is unfair and bitterly cruel to train a child to be fat just because you cannot discipline your own desires for food. You, as a parent and adult, set the example for the eating habits in your home.

Reprogramming Your Life-style

Many overweight people are led to believe that they need not fear their corpulence because they are one of those people who need to be fat to be able to cope with all of life's problems. This is not "coping," it's "copping out," hiding behind their problem rather than facing it. I have never seen a case where a previously fat person could not cope much better after he became thinner, if he lost his weight in a healthy manner.

Overweight problems and their treatment have moved from sound nutrition, good eating habits and exercise, to the psychiatrist's couch, diet pills, shots, and the emotional dialogue found in popular magazines. There is a simple way to lose weight—simple but not necessarily easy. You can lose weight and you can do it without all the modern props. You already have all the necessary tools within you. But first you must decide if you want to be the master or slave of your own body!

Your brain controls all that goes on in your body, giving orders consciously and unconsciously. It is your will that changes the physical condition of your body, for muscles and appetites do not have minds of their own. They may become accustomed to a certain kind of food or physical activity or lack of it.

But if you really want to lose weight, *desperate* to lose weight, your habits are changeable. You can reprogram your life-style.

Too many people decide from the start that they just can't lose weight, that they lack the stick-to-itiveness. But anyone, even someone with very little personal drive, can adopt the program on the following pages and get fantastic results. No gimmicks, no magic, just results.

Everyone likes to picture himself as his own boss, fully in control of his own decisions. This is a good personality trait, especially in the complicated, superorganized world in which we live. We need to maintain the sovereignty of personal initiative. This applies most profoundly to our bodies.

Picture your body as a computer. What you program it to do, it does. Decisions are not at all unpredictable for they are based on material input. Your mind is the memory bank for your body, receiving impulses and information from outside sources and retaining *all* of it. Everything you do, say, think, see and hear is filed away within your mind.

20

The Thin Person Inside Your Fat One

The main difference between your body and computers is the God-given prerogative of freedom of choice. From the data you receive, you can choose what you wish to do or say or think or be. *Yes, to be!* Unlike any other creature you can change the shape and size of your body. If you are overweight you can lose. If you are underweight you can gain. If you wish to be a little more muscular or gain some muscular size, you can do it. Your physical body is like a pile of clay that can be molded or shaped as you see fit. You have heard that whatever the mind of man can believe he can conceive. This is absolutely true. Regardless of who has counseled you to the contrary, *you can lose weight.*

If you sincerely want to lose weight and keep it off, come along, I'll show you how. For those who have never traveled the modern road to Thindom, I welcome your interest and promise you more than you bargained for.

chapter two
What Is Food?

It probably sounds silly to be asking, What is food? For food, obviously, is everything we eat. Products we buy in the grocery store, items we eat at restaurants, special treats from ice-cream trucks, or delicious snacks from drive-thru, quick-eating establishments.

Food is the convenience of a whole dinner ready packaged in a pretty container, popped into a preheated oven for 35 minutes and served.

Food is the businessman's breakfast—coffee and roll.

Food is the two cups of refined sugar we Americans consume daily.

Food is the low-calorie drinks for those of us on diets.

Food includes all those "goodies" the food industry and its advertising specialists convince us we want and need.

Food is all the preservatives, flavorings, chemical additives—and who knows what else—that are dumped down our throats by the food technologists.

Food! Sure, we all know what it is. We consume it every day. Food is any substance which can be put in the mouth, digested, and used to feed and nourish the body. Food is the only source of raw material that supplies the fuel, building material, repair material and necessary vitamins, minerals, and other trace elements which help our body function in the most efficient manner. In other words, food enables the body to stay alive, and the better quality food, the better quality body. But are we really aware of what is in the food products we buy? Do we have any idea what has been done to the *basic seven food groups*? Is the quality of food what it should be?

Do I mean to suggest that some things we eat are not food? That is exactly what I mean. These items I call *non-food*. They do absolutely nothing in a positive manner for our bodies. They merely fatten the pocketbooks of unscrupulous manufacturers and often harm the customers.

The introduction of *non-food* into the American diet is a product of modern food technology and the illegitimate offspring of many chemists who try to make life a little easier by giving us convenient meals. But they are not totally to blame, for they simply supply a service which is in demand.

Today we suffer health problems by the bushels-full. Sickness and disease seem to be the rule rather than the exception. Why is the United States number 1 in wealth and number 23 in health? Why is cancer so common? Why do we encounter such a high incidence of degenerative diseases such as arthritis and osteoporosis? Why is so much effort going into finding a cure for the common cold? Why are stomach and digestion problems, such as poor elimination and irregularity, the number one type of complaint to doctors?

The twentieth century is the nuclear age, rich in scientific knowledge. We know how to harness the atom and make it work for us. We have walked on the moon. We can travel from one part of the earth to another in a matter of hours. In this complex world, progress is measured in weeks or months, not years or decades.

But with all this progress we still possess minimal knowledge about bodily functions and how we can attain and maintain a healthy life. In fact this age of specialization has contributed to our body ignorance, for we are lulled into believing that our medical fathers can tell us how to stay healthy and, if need be, how to lose weight. Many of us feel incompetent to attack our overweight problems by ourselves. "Seek help from a doctor," we are told. "If anyone knows anything about the body, it must be a doctor. Look at his years of study." All this is true, but how many doctors have studied preventive medicine in general and common sense health habits in particular?

Doctors are so busy that they often do not have the time or inclination to move from their speciality to a general problem like overweight. So you must take the initiative yourself. You can, without medical help, take off and keep off that extra, ugly weight. As a starting point, you must take inventory of your personal habits and life pattern, beginning with what enters your mouth.

Avoid Convenience Foods

Our accelerated life-styles create many problems, one of which relates to our rushing hither and thither so that we do not have time to sit down and enjoy our meals. Technologists have designed ready-prepared products that take little or no time to cook and can be gobbled down quickly. The convenience of these chemical concoctions is their *only* endearing quality. Many times they resemble, in appearance and taste, the nutritious food we are accustomed to. But that is where the similarity ends. Oh yes, there is food in these products, but they are so loaded with *non-foods* you would almost be better off not eating at all.

Convenience is an attitude for the mind, not for the body. Whether you are in a hurry or not, your body still requires fuel just as a car does. Substitutes will not suffice. It is unfortunate, in a way, that our bodies do not react to poor material input as a car does. For when we "misfeed" a car the results are quick and predictable. But the effects may not become evident in our bodies for a long time.

This chemical bombardment is of our own making, and so we can change it. But *we* must be the one to act. The food technologists certainly will not. They are interested in your money, not your health.

Many of the modern convenient eating items present an added danger. The different chemicals and *non-food-stuffs* are put together to taste palatable; but they are addicting. We return to them because of a certain flavor or taste which technologists know we will like and like again. Sugar is one of the worst offenders. We will consider sugar shortly, but suffice it to say that these convenient, addicting *non-food* products encourage repeat customers by virtue of their taste, not their content.

Two generations ago Americans lived a different kind of life. The population was largely rural and we enjoyed a slower pace. It was not uncommon to see a man, not a farmer but a white collar worker, spending his free hours toiling in the soil, growing fruits and vegetables for pleasure and consumption.

Growing his own food not only provided better nutrition, but man also received therapeutic value from the activity. We acquire a special kind of calmness when earth and hands meet. We receive a sense of achieve-

25

ment from seeing things grow that we plant and care for; a feeling of personal worth so lacking in big-city life where frustration is the watchword.

Besides gaining nutritional, emotional and spiritual benefits in his own garden, man learned firsthand about growing plants, feeding animals and recognizing cycles and balances of nature that affected him. He could observe the results when he tampered with the natural diets of animals and the environments of plants. In this way likewise he understood that the human body is a living organism, not a chemistry set. I tend to think this earlier man was more aware of the worth of life in relation to monetary success. He understood that wealth amounted to very little if he didn't have health.

Learn Food Selection

Developing skills in selecting food may seem far removed from the problem of losing weight, but it is not. Selecting what you eat is the beginning of making a new, slimmer, healthier you.[1]

We are told that, in one year, 98 percent of all the atoms in our cells is replaced by new atoms. New atoms, new cells, new body.[2] If this is the case, we must certainly focus clearly upon our eating habits, consuming the best quality food available and cutting the non-food from our menu. Chemicals and assorted flavorings do not feed the body, only *food* does. And better food creates a better body.

Whatever you eat, first ask, "What will this do for me or to me?" Your diet—your food intake—must satisfy the daily needs of your body, *every day*. Your body is not something you send on vacation while you starve yourself for a month to lose those last few pounds for the bikini season. If your diet is so unbalanced or drastically lacking in vital elements that you crave sweets, or if, when you go off your diet, you gain all your weight back plus more, or if you become so mentally miserable that you snap at everyone around you, then your selection of nutritious body-building foods is not satisfying your normal body needs. Careful food selection will enable you to lose weight. This is not theory but a realistic and attainable goal.

Become a Label Reader

To make those wise food selections, you need to become a *label reader*. This activity may not be as interesting as reading a new novel, but it promises fantastic benefits. Many of us, unfortunately, buy products according to name brand; however, we don't eat the name but the product. So when you enter the local shopping center to purchase your family's food, do not buy anything until you *closely* read that label. Find out what your money is purchasing—*food or fake.*

Label reading is an art. Manufacturers are very clever in preparing and placing their labels; thus you must look a product over very closely when determining what is inside. The colorful packaging or design may almost obliterate the label, or the ingredients panel may be printed in such small type that, even after you find the label, it is difficult to read. Label makers do this for a reason. Many of the ingredients found in our modern products are not food at all but different non-nutritive chemicals. So clever label placing often hides these additives under the guise of an attractive package. Search out the label and assure yourself that what you are buying is real, not artificial. For example, the contents label of a commercial breakfast cereal reads: milled corn, sugar, salt, malt flavoring, sodium ascorbate, vitamin A palmitate, niacinamide, zinc oxide, pyridoxine hydrochloride, folic acid, Vitamin D_2, BHA and BHT. A commercial chocolate cream pie reads: sodium caseinate, sugar, lecithin, monocalcium phosphate, calcium oxide, mono-diglycerides, sodium phosphate, cellulose gum, polysorbate 60, artificial color.

What do you look for in your label reading campaign? What ingredients should you avoid?

Chemical flavorings: This notable group of artificial flavorings are used in some products to make the synthetic or non-food items palatable that would normally be too distasteful to eat. These chemicals add nothing to the nutritional value of any food. In fact, many chemical flavorings have been accused of causing or contributing to harmful side effects. Chemical flavorings fool you by attracting your taste buds, but supply no nutrients. The product tastes good, so you buy it again.

Some typical chemical flavorings you might find on contents labels are: sorbitol, saccharin, acetic acid, acetone, benzoic acid, BHA, BHT, caffeine, camphor, caramel, citric acid, decanol, formic acid, glutamic acid, piperonal, salicylic acid, tannic acid, valeric acid, vanillin.

Don't let taste become the primary criterion for product purchase. Your body knows the nutritional difference between the natural food flavor of oranges or honey and saccharin or cyclamates. The natural flavorings in food have their purpose in feeding the body. Fruit flavors are usually carbohydrates, and carbohydrates are fuel, supplying us with energy.

It is interesting to note that the danger of chemical additives and flavorings in our food has been recognized for a long time. Dr. Harvey W. Wiley, the founder of the FDA (Food and Drug Administration, the government-appointed guardian of the consumer), as far back as the 1920s, warned against the danger of saccharin and presented test results concerning its harmful effects on animals. And yet, 60 years later, saccharin, a coal tar product, is still the largest sugar substitute on the market. (Controversy linking saccharin with cancer is raging at this time.) If saccharin is dangerous, why has it remained on the market? Why hasn't a safe sugar substitute been developed? Primarily because it makes a large group of people a great deal of money. The almighty dollar, not nutrition or health, motivates most of the food industry. [3]

Saccharin and other chemical additive flavorings were originally used because they cost less than the natural flavors and the calorie content was much lower. Dieters are usually obsessed with keeping their calories down. What is a calorie? A calorie is a unit of activity. The more calories you consume the more energy your body has. If you do not use up all the calories in energy, however, you will add the extra to your body as fat. So you should be conscious of the amount of calories you consume. But more important, you should be conscious of the *kind* of calories you consume. Food calories supply energy; chemical calories do not.

So even though chemical sweeteners may have fewer calories than the natural sweeteners found in food, these fewer calories have no value whatsoever for the body. They don't even satisfy your craving for something sweet. Honey or fresh fruit satisfies your sweet taste. Chemical sweeteners are many times sweeter than natural ones—saccharin is almost 300 to 500 times sweeter —but they do not provide food value.

Food manufacturers or the FDA demonstrate little concern over the effects chemical additives have on your metabolism or the delicate nutritional balance of your body. So, since the food industry and the public's product protectors do so little to eliminate the chemical additives from your food, you must do so yourself.

When you buy that 12-ounce soft drink with only one calorie, be conscious that the product is 12 ounces of chemicals. Besides, this 12-ounce chemical concoction takes the place of nutritious, healthy food, which may be higher in calories but is also higher in food value. Your body is not as easily fooled as your tastebuds are.

Read labels and stay away from products that contain artificial flavorings.

Preservatives: Preservatives are another contribution from the food industry. When we were a country of largely rural population areas, we had the opportunity to eat fresh fruits, vegetables and meat. We could consume foods that were still fresh because they were grown close to us. Simple life, simple food—taken out of the ground, off the trees, from the slaughterhouse and into our homes.

As our country expanded from rural to urban, problems in getting fresh, wholesome food from farm to city precipitated the invention of food preservatives. Chemicals kept certain foods from going bad as quickly as they normally would. Preservatives themselves add nothing to the value of the food. Actually they do harm because they allow you to eat foods that would already have gone bad without them. Here is an old proverb worth remembering: "Don't eat anything that won't rot, spoil, or mildew. Just eat it before it does." When you read on the labels that the food you are considering contains chemicals such as BHA and BHT, two chemicals also found in embalming fluid, do yourself a favor. Preserve your body by passing up the foods with preservatives.

Other Chemical Additives: Another silent danger in our modern food selection concerns the problem of chemical residues in food. Vegetables and fruits are often waxed and colored to hide their age and increase their eye appeal. This is alarming, but there is something

30

worse. I am referring specifically to the way most fruits and vegetables are now grown. Farmers use high nitrogen, chemical type fertilizers to produce larger crops. These chemical fertilizers "blow-up" the size of the plants and upset the mineral balance of the soil. Fruits and vegetables manufacture their own vitamins but their minerals must come from the soil in which they are grown. Plants nurtured on mineral-deficient farmlands produce mineral-lacking fruits and vegetables.[4]

In the process of tampering with the soil the farmer also bombards his crops with many kinds of pesticides and insecticides, poisons designed to kill all potential insect and bacterial invaders. These poisons, however, also create a real danger to the consumer. You stand an excellent chance of getting small concentrations of some very deadly poisons.

This situation has not gone unnoticed by federal and state governments. DDT, until recently a widely-used bug killer, has long been recognized as a very dangerous poison for man because once ingested it collects in the fatty tissues of the body and *cannot be eliminated*. The amounts in any one food may be very small, but the danger lurks in its cumulative effects.

But how can you, as a consumer, protect your family against this type of poisoning?

Organic Gardening

A popular movement today calls for a return to farming as it used to be done. This is called *organic farming*. Organically grown fruits and vegetables are those which have been planted in soils enriched with fertilizer of plant or animal origin. This type of fertilizer, without chemicals, naturally enriches the soil and builds up its mineral content.

Also in organic gardening no pesticides or poisonous

31

sprays are used. The organic farmer relies on the natural balance of nature—an acid-rich soil plus insect predators equal healthy plants. Until a few years ago this is how we farmed, taking from the land and putting our wastes back into the land to rebuild the soil we used.

In our search for organic produce we encounter problems because there is no legal definition for "organic" as it pertains to growing food. (One exception, Oregon legally defines "organic farming" the way we do in this section.) Many people put forth a variety of definitions. Several times I have tried to buy what was advertised as organically-grown fruits or vegetables only to discover that the retailer and I possessed contrasting definitions for the same word. This allows for considerable confusion and outright dishonesty. I have noted that even some health food stores sell regular produce at a higher price and claim it was organically grown.

In your search for nonpolluted fruits and vegetables, you will be most satisfied if you grow your own. In that way you can be sure of what you are eating for you will know what you put in the soil, what you put on the plants, and when your produce was picked.

The only other alternative is that you investigate the source of your fruits and vegetables, if possible, and actually see how they are grown. Any reputable firm will welcome your interest. If this is impractical, you can at least attempt to clarify the retailer's definition of organic and then rely on his honesty.

This may seem like excessive effort to most housewives, and it is. But the results are a better quality food supply for your family. Just as preservatives, chemical flavorings and additives do not feed the body, chemical residues from modern farming interfere with proper assimilation of foods. They may not kill you today but they could certainly shorten your life.

32

As a concerned consumer I have prepared the following chart of some typical *non-foods* and corresponding *foods*. In the next few chapters we will take a stroll through our modern supermarkets and health food stores and identify some popularly consumed *non-foods* and explain what dangers they present to us. With the elimination of a *non-food* we will replace it with a good, high quality, unadulterated food.

Common Sense Guide to Wise Food Selection

Non-food	*Food*
Refined Sugar	Honey
Coffee	Juices, Herb Teas
White Bread	Whole Wheat
Commercial Cereals	Whole Grain Cereals
Ice Cream	Honey Ice Cream
Soft Drinks	Fruit & Vegetable Juices
Diet Drinks	Juices or Milk
Commercial Seasonings	Vegetable Salt or Sea Salt
Chocolate	Carob
Alcohol	Juices or Milk
Cigarettes	Air

Notes

1. J.I. Rodale, *The Health Seekers* (Emmaus, Penn.: Rodale Press, Inc., 1971), p. 19.
2. Linda Clark, *Stay Young Longer* (New York: Pyramid Publications, 1968), p. 30.
3. In J.I. Rodale's *Our Poisoned Earth and Sky* (Emmaus, Penn: Rodale Press, Inc., 1964), on pages 100 and 101, several research studies are mentioned which detail the harmful effects of saccharin in food. Saccharin is not a food. It is a non-food and does not belong in your body. The controversy over saccharin in the seventies is not over whether it is harmful or not harmful, but rather whether vested money interests will once again pull a fast one on uninformed and often gullible public. We should be informed about the most widely consumed artificial sweetener.
4. Rodale, *Our Poisoned Earth*, pp. 184,185.

part two

Foods and Non-foods

chapter three
Sugar and Spice

chapter four
Don't Drink to That

chapter five
The Staff of Life

chapter six
Satisfying Your Sweet Tooth

chapter seven
Smoke Gets in Your Eyes— And Everywhere Else

chapter three
Sugar and Spice

When I was a young boy, I can remember going to the Saturday afternoon matinee to see the cowboy serials. Each Saturday the episode would end with the hero in a very dangerous situation, thus demanding a return visit the following Saturday to see how the hero would escape. The plot was always the same, the good guys against the bad guys, two forces easily identifiable even without dialogue. The good guys in white, the bad guys in black.

We seem to have carried over this color coding of good and bad into our everyday living, even into the selections of what we choose to eat. Unfortunately, white bread and white sugar are looked upon by many people as the "good guys," the things to buy. However, unadulterated, life-giving food comes in many colors; but, except for eggs, seldom in white.

Refined Sugar, a *Non-food*

Non-food items take many shapes and forms, but none is more prevalent or dangerous than refined sugar. Refined sugar is any sugar that has been removed from a food, separated from its vitamins, minerals and enzymes, and added to a product or sold by itself. As much as 65 percent of all foods in our friendly grocery store contain some kind of refined sugar. A check of the labels reveals such names as sucrose, dextrose, maltose, fructose, glucose, lactose, brown sugar, Yellow-D sugar, washed raw sugar, turbinado raw sugar, corn syrup, raisin syrup, grape sugar, and a few others. It is important to remember that these are *all* refined sugars when they appear on the label of a product as a flavoring.

Fructose is fruit sugar, the natural sugar found in fruits. White sugar comes from sugar cane or sugar beets, two nutritious foods. However, when the food processors get their hands on these foods, they strip them—the sugars—of all the vitamins, minerals, and enzymes necessary for proper digestion. These are the very elements your body must supply if they are lacking in your food. Thus the body must rob itself to supply the missing ingredients. Fruits, vegetables and dairy products are good examples of foods that supply sugar as well as the elements necessary for their digestion. In fact, all *foods* that contain sugar also have these important digestive elements.

Refined sugar is added to many foods because of its taste. It is extremely concentrated and very sweet, sometimes sickly sweet. When we eat a piece of fruit, the natural sugar and associates (vitamins, minerals, and enzymes) satisfy our taste buds' sweet inclination and

37

nutritionally fill the body's requests for energy. The food chain of vitamins, minerals, carbohydrates and enzymes in fruit completely feed the body.

Recently I was eating in a Los Angeles restaurant. Being in a hurry, I didn't take the time to be as choosy as usual in picking a place to eat. Feeling my blood sugar level getting low and a medium-sized headache coming on, I ordered a large salad and a chicken dinner. I often enjoy a good salad before my meal, for it starts my digestive juices flowing and prepares me for the meal ahead. I normally use a vinegar and oil dressing that my wife makes. This particular day I decided to take a chance on a commercial dressing. I think they said it was French dressing. You may not be aware of it, but all the usual salad dressings that you buy in stores or eat in restaurants are loaded with refined sugar.

As I ate my salad, a strange thing happened. My taste buds seemed to be anesthetized by the dressing. That is, my taste grew duller as I ate and I found a craving for the salad with the dressing. I was not satisfied with the normal amount of salad, and I gorged myself on more salad until I had no appetite for the main course. I am not presenting this as an accredited laboratory experiment; but I am convinced the refined sugar in the salad dressing jaded my appetite and created my craving for more salad with the sugared dressing.

Refined sugar contains no B-vitamins. B-vitamins are necessary to digest sugar. B-vitamins break down protein food into amino acids. Amino acids are the building blocks of your body. They are responsible for your growth and for repairing your body. Since refined sugar has no B-vitamins in it, your body must supply these water-soluble vitamins to digest the sugar; therefore, refined sugar robs your body of its vital supply. When you eat any kind of protein, whether it's steak or eggs or protein powder, and at the same time drink a low-sugared drink, you waste a significant amount, if not most, of this important protein food.

Refined sugar blocks the proper assimilation of calcium. Calcium, in order to be digested, must encounter an acid environment in your stomach. Refined sugar changes the acid environment to alkaline so that your stomach cannot fully digest the calcium. You either pass it through your system or it tends to form calcium deposits in the parts of your body you use most: hands, feet, shoulders, etc.[1]

Many adults believe they no longer need calcium after they reach adulthood, but this is simply not true. Bones, like all other tissues in the body, are living organisms. Old cells continually die and new cells form to replace them. If you do not get sufficient calcium in your diet to repair muscle tissue, heal injured parts, conduct nerve impulses and many other functions, where will your body find this essential mineral? It takes calcium from the calcium bank account—your bones. Over 98 percent of body calcium is stored inside our bones.[2] But these calcium stores are not unlimited. When reserves of calcium are used up, your bones can become brittle and begin to fall apart. An elderly person who falls and breaks his hip, for instance, reaps the expected harvest from a calcium-deficient diet or from eating, for too many years, foods that are heavily polluted with refined sugar. His hip didn't really break, it disintegrated!

When I was counseling at a Jack LaLanne Health Spa several years ago, an attractive middle-aged woman visited me at the nutrition center. She had just joined the spa on the advice of her doctor. A short time before she had slipped on her porch and broken her hip. Her physician suggested that light exercise and the therapy pool would aid in her recovery. X-rays of her broken hip showed that the hip joint was very low in calcium. The doctor told her that she would be burdened with this weak hip the rest of her life. He didn't ask about her eating habits.

I discovered that Ann was a heavy coffee drinker, a sweet eater, a very erratic nibbler and consumed very little calcium in her diet. After we talked, she eliminated coffee, sugar and other *non-foods*. She developed a consistent eating pattern and started to include calcium-rich foods and a calcium supplement in her diet. Within two weeks her fingernails, which always split when they reached a certain length (not even gelatin could help), were strong, hard and more attractive than they had ever been. Within six months her constant bone aches disappeared and X-rays of her shattered hip showed massive deposits of new calcium. She was recovering from the condition that caused her shattered hip.

The moral: keep your calcium intake high and eliminate refined sugars and your body won't have to overdraw from its calcium bank.

Refined sugars lead to cholesterol buildup in your arteries. We hear much today about cholesterol building in the arterial walls. Cholesterol leads to hardening of the arteries, high blood pressure and possible heart attacks. Refined sugars are carbohydrates, and carbohydrates are readily converted into fats and can easily be stored in the lining of the arteries. Read those labels and eliminate all refined sugars. Just a teaspoon a day won't hurt, you say. No, but how about a teaspoon a day for 40 or 50 years? Please remember also that the average consumption of refined sugar per person is close to *100 pounds a year*. Accumulation of fat and constant depletion of important nutrients are real dangers in the consumption of refined sugar.

I could spend many pages on the effects of refined

sugar, all of which are negative. But many books have been written on this subject and I refer you to them for more information and technical data. I just wish to impress upon you that refined sugar is one item that does not belong in your food. It isn't conducive to good health. Does this mean then that you can have no sweetening for your foods? Certainly not.

Honey, Rich in Potassium

Raw honey is probably the best sweetener that you can add to any food and it contains all the necessary properties for healthy digestion. A little bit of honey, unlike refined sugar which sets up a craving for more sugar, provides more lasting satisfaction. It takes very little to satisfy even the strongest sweet tooth. Honey can be added in cooking just like refined sugar, but normally you need only half the amount.

One of the most important components in honey is the mineral potassium, which has lately become a crowd-pleaser for the overweight group. Potassium is the fluid policeman for the body. Excess fluid in your body provides a fertile breeding ground for all sorts of bacteria invaders. Fluid also adds weight to your body and, therefore, strain to your already overworked heart.[3] Potassium maintains healthy levels of body fluid and aids in removing excess fluids. Many folk remedies utilize honey for this very purpose. If excess fluid is one of your problems, honey can be more effective than diuretic pills and less dangerous to your system.

I will not attempt to sound authoritative on a subject which some people have spent their whole lives investigating. Suffice it to say that honey should replace refined sugars because honey contains B-vitamins, minerals and enzymes necessary for digestion. Therefore, honey aids the digestion of other foods.

MSG Is Not A-OK

Oriental food is quite popular nowadays, especially because of all the steamed vegetables that are normally served. Chinese and Japanese restaurants, once rare, are now quite common. Have you ever noticed how spicy and sharp tasting many of the dishes are? This is not the normal bland or nearly bland taste of these foods. American-Oriental restaurants are utilizing yet another chemical marvel, this time in the area of food seasonings: monosodium glutamate or MSG.

Our taste conscious society craves food that tastes good. We are usually more concerned with a certain product's taste than with its ingredients. Is it food? Is it chemical? Will it feed my body?

Next to refined sugar, MSG appears in more foods than any other chemical additive. Label reading will once again expose this ingredient. Canned soups, many frozen vegetables, stews, treats, and a large number of other products contain monosodium glutamate. Incidentally, for those of you with good nutritional book knowledge, a compound called monosodium glutamate is found in the human brain. But this is a different substance than that which food chemists use in food. The brain MSG is a by-product of brain activity and comes from the digestion of food. The MSG used in food seasonings is *non-food* composed of chemicals made in a test tube. Such chemicals don't feed a living body.

One of the most prominent offenses of MSG pertains to your digestion. Scientists have known for a long time that MSG interferes with the proper digestion of food. Many people eating commercial Oriental foods, which contain high amounts of MSG, have come away from their meals with indigestion, gas, intestinal pain, headaches or nausea. If you use MSG regularly and have not suffered any distress, you are more fortunate than most.

Thank your parents and grandparents for your healthy constitution, but don't abuse it by continually chemicalizing with MSG. Stay away from this *non-food*. It deserves no place in a diet for losing weight and gaining health. In fact you will find that your food tastes so much better without the chemical helps.

A Word about Salt

The other popular spicer is table salt. I have observed people in restaurants pour salt on their food before even tasting it. Salt, like MSG, is addicting. It so anesthetizes our taste buds that we seem to need more of it every time to enjoy our food. This is evidence of the drug-like effect of table salt on the body.

Table salt, not the same as sea salt, is made by combining two chemicals, sodium and chlorine. These chemicals, which appear in many *non-food* items, will not feed the body. The sodium and chlorine found in sea salt occur naturally. Sea salt is dried salt water, capable of feeding the body. Of special interest, chemists have been able to identify all the elements found in sea water and make synthetic salt water. The only problem is that salt water fish can live in salt water but not in synthetic salt water. The elements are exactly the same but something is missing.

Many reasons exist for keeping salt intake down, but the most important one concerns its effect on water retention. The more salt we consume the greater amount of excess fluid our bodies will retain. The sodium in salt, we discover, replaces the potassium to a great extent in the body. Potassium is that mineral which has a mild diuretic effect on body fluids. As the potassium lowers, excess fluid rises. The more fluid we carry, the more liquids we retain for bacteria growth. I am speaking now of disease-carrying bacteria. Bacteria need moisture to maintain their strength in your body. Cut back on excess fluids and cut down on breeding grounds for sickness.

Excess fluid also puts a tremendous strain on the heart, which must pump harder to get the blood-carrying nutrients to the different parts of the body that are being cramped by this extra weight. We need to take it easy on our heart as far as unnecessary work is concerned. Why waste its vital strength?

In applying salt to food, use it sparingly. And by all means, instead of table salt use sea salt. Instead of monosodium glutamate, use vegetable salt, available in most health stores, which is a little sea salt combined with dehydrated vegetables. The taste is really fantastic and you are ingesting legitimate food. Read your labels and abstain from these chemically-doctored products manufactured to please the taste and not the body.

One more thing on table salt. When you pick up a container of table salt, check the ingredient panel. Most table salt now contains dextrose, a refined sugar made from corn. Again, *non-food*.

Notes

1. J.I. Rodale, *Health Builders* (Emmaus, Penn.: Rodale Press, Inc., 1957), p. 425.
2. Ibid, p. 107.
3. E.H. Jarvis, *Arthritis and Folk Medicine* (New York: Fawcett World Library, 1960).

chapter four

Don't Drink to That

Nowhere is the effect of monster technology more evident than in the liquids we drink. More chemicals and *non-foods* slide down our throats in drinks and mixes than almost any other group of products. Modern refreshments can taste so good and be so bad. Our only defense against these *non-foods* is to read labels. Taste alone should not and cannot be the sole reason for consuming any beverage. Man may chemically duplicate food drinks that taste like the real thing, but they are imitations. Man cannot duplicate the nutritious elements and health-giving food factors found in natural liquid food.

The Ritual Coffee Break

I now begin to tread on many Americans' toes. Few

rituals seem as sacred as the businessman's morning cup of coffee or the proverbial coffee break. Again we must class coffee as a *non-food*. Coffee has no nutritional value whatsoever, nothing to feed the body or supply it with any necessary food element. And yet we consume it by the gallon.

When he learns that his favorite drink is not good for him, Sam Citizen inevitably exclaims, "But everybody drinks it, so how can it be bad? I've never heard of anyone dying from an overdose of coffee." Fortunately for us, the body is a wonderful organism. It can take the abuses we heap upon it year upon year without uttering a complaint. But eventually, we will begin to recognize the damage we have done.

Coffee is a stimulant. Years ago cardiologists recognized that caffeine could be used to stimulate the heartbeat of patients whose damaged hearts were slowing down due to the strain of heart disease. But the average heart does not need this stimulation. Caffeine in coffee can pose a danger to an otherwise healthy heart.

Endangering the heart isn't the only problem coffee drinkers should beware of. In my opinion, coffee is the number one cause of hypoglycemia—low blood sugar. In the last 10 years, more literature has been devoted to the subject of hypoglycemia than any other health problem we have produced. Yes, we *produce* hypoglycemia.

The pancreas is the organ that regulates the amount of sugar in the bloodstream. When you eat or drink anything, food or *non-food*, your body begins to function as if you are ingesting nutrients. Your liver releases glycogen, protein that has been converted into carbohydrate to be used later for energy, and converts it into glucose. When you drink a cup of coffee your body sends messages to the pancreas that food is now being consumed and your body begins its digestive processes.

46

Your body cannot tell whether the increased sugar in your blood came from food that you ate or from glycogen your liver released. So your pancreas produces insulin, its special enzyme, to take any excess sugar from your bloodstream. However, because there is no food value in coffee—only caffeine and a little glycogen—your blood sugar level goes down. In this way you force your blood sugar level to continually dip drastically low by bombarding your pancreas with coffee. If you do this on a regular basis, your pancreas will continually overreact, keeping your blood sugar level, and consequently your energy level, at a very low point.

Bill was a hardworking upper-level executive in a Los Angeles-based aerospace corporation. His job required long hours and was packed from early morning to late evening with more pressure and demands than most men can even begin to handle. He hardly had time to eat and he gulped down whatever was available. Coffee was his main staple. For over 10 years he skipped breakfast, ran through lunch, gorged himself at dinner and drank 10 to 20 cups of coffee a day. When I first met him he was experiencing severe periods of depression, jittery nerves, consistent shortness of temper and a general listlessness. Many mornings he found it hard to get out of bed. His head throbbed and only his morning cups of coffee got him out the door.

Stomach pains sent Bill to his doctor who told him that his condition sounded like the beginning of a stomach ulcer, not uncommon to someone in Bill's position. The doctor prescribed medicine, told him to avoid certain foods, and suggested he take it a little easier. Bill followed these instructions and started an exercise program, and soon began to have a little relief. But he still suffered light-headedness, irritability and a lack of concentration.

We changed his eating habits drastically, took him off *non-foods* and eliminated *all* coffee from his diet. The results were dramatic. He slept better, had no coffee hangovers in the morning, his irritability decreased and his drive increased. He had more energy than he had had in years. The coffee was beating him to death.

You cannot solve the problem of hypoglycemia by eating eight to ten meals a day—you only treat the symptom. You didn't become hypoglycemic because you failed to eat 8 or 10 meals a day but rather, in part, because coffee and other *non-foods* have been over-stimulating your pancreas. If you depend on the 10 o'clock coffee break to give you an energy boost after a busy morning, it is like beating a tired horse. Coffee stimulates your body with a drug, not with food.

Caffeine destroys the B-vitamins that are important for a healthy, calm nervous system.[1] One of the B-vitamins, choline, is a constituent in the enzyme cholinase, which is very critical for the normal transfer of electrical impulses up and down the spinal column. If your nervous system is low in this enzyme cholinase, the myelin sheath—the nerve covering—will not protect the nerve endings nor provide the conduction for nerve impulses. These nerve impulses are like electrical impulses. Without healthy conductors this energy can be short-circuited and inconsistent. Coffee, with caffein, will make your nervous system ineffective.

Coffee jitters are not imagination but the cold, hard results of caffeine addiction. *Addiction!* The longer you drink coffee, the more you will need to drink to gain the same effects. Because your body develops a tolerance for the drug, an added dosage is required to provide the increase in energy—otherwise known as the "shot in the arm." Our society is alarmingly filled with many 10 to 20 cups-of-coffee-a-day people.

48

Coffee dilutes digestive juices. Digestive juices are the main ingredients for proper and complete digestion of all the food we eat. We frequently hear the admonition, "You are what you eat." This is not quite true. *You are what you digest from what you eat.* "Digest" is the key word. Your diet may be the best in the world, but if you insist on pouring coffee into your stomach, you may be missing a large amount of the nutritional benefits from your food. Undigested foods are either eliminated as waste or stored as fat. The B-vitamins, extremely rich in the digestive juices, are manufactured by the body in the intestinal tract and take part in the digestion of nearly all foods we consume. But we have little hope for a bumper crop of B-vitamins when we continually "water" them with coffee.

Three cups of coffee a day use up three cups worth of stomach space. Let us pretend, for argument's sake, that your stomach can hold a quart of liquid and solid food every three or four hours. The overweight person is very conscious of how much he eats, so trading coffee for food makes good calorie sense, and besides the caffeine imparts temporary energy. Meanwhile his body is being deprived of the nutrients it needs daily.

I know many coffee drinkers who protest that they are merely enjoying a hot drink in the morning. For some reason they overlook the other hot drinks that do not contain the offending caffeine. There is only 100 milligrams of caffeine in a cup of coffee, but how powerful it is. This caffeine is the main ingredient in nonprescription pep pills. If you have ever resorted to one of these drugs on a long driving trip or used them to give you an extra amount of alertness during a period of exhaustion, no one need tell you the kind of stimulation they provide.

Many coffee drinkers, realizing the unhealthy side

effects of caffeine, are switching to decaffeinated coffee. However, you are still getting some caffeine. Add to this the dangerous chemicals the processors use to decaffeinate the coffee—the residues of which can remain in the coffee you drink, and you still have an excellent reason to omit this liquid from your body. As long as one-half of one percent of caffeine remains in coffee you should not drink it. As long as coffee contains no nutritional benefits, it is a *non-food* and you should not drink it.

Just one more comment: Over 20 years ago researchers found that when coffee was roasted the heat produced coffee tars, similar in appearance to cigarette tars. These unbiased scientific researchers felt coffee consumption could be directly related to peptic ulcers and stomach cancer. *Non-food* is non-health.

If you insist on having something warm to drink for breakfast, try herb teas. They do not contain caffeine but do provide vitamins, minerals and other food factors. If hot drinks are not important to you, many unsweetened fruit juices will get your motor running in the morning. Fruit juices are high in carbohydrates but contain food factors missing in refined sugar. A word of warning here. All juices which say "sweetened" on the label have been sweetened with some kind of refined sugar. It is not necessary to sweeten a juice that is already naturally sweet.

Soft Drinks—Treat or Trick

Twentieth-century living has brought us another modern invention from the food technologist. It's hard to imagine having a Saturday afternoon picnic, enjoying a breezy yachting adventure, or relaxing after any sport or activity without "enjoying" one of today's popular soft drinks. The advertising is enormous. But what do these soft drinks contain?

I frequently wonder how manufacturers get away with calling these concoctions "soft drinks"; they are not in the least bit soft.

Soft drinks are extremely acidic. The fact that soft drinks irritate the soft tissues in the stomach and intestinal tract may partially explain why the number one complaint to doctors is stomach problems. Soft drinks contain phosphoric acid, which damages the delicate stomach lining and thereby interferes with the normal secretion of digestive juices and enzymes necessary for the proper digestion, assimilation and rearrangement of food elements into whatever the body needs to fulfill its nutritional requirements for maintenance, repair, and good health.

Soft drinks contain carbonated water. Carbonated water is a combination of carbon dioxide and water. A normal waste product thrown off by our body after food is digested, carbon dioxide is a food for plants but not for man. It supplies the bubbly, effervescent qualities featured in our soft drinks; chemicals manipulated expertly to satisfy our taste buds.

Soft drinks are sweetened with refined sugar—cheap to add but costly in its addiction. When you tell yourself, "Boy, wouldn't a nice glass of #%&*#$% go good right now," you have been reeled in by the advertiser's line and have swallowed the chemists' drugs. I have never heard one doctor, nutritionist, chemist or advertising man say that #%&*#$% or UN-#%&*#$% offers anything nutritionally positive for the body. They tell us it won't hurt us, and they are absolutely right. It won't hurt you or me if we don't drink it. It is *non-food*, so leave it alone.

Most standard weight loss books include soft drinks in their diet recommendations. You will not find them in this one for you should be concerned about keeping your health while you are losing weight. Soft drinks take valuable space in your stomach which is better filled with fruit or vegetable juices. Soft drinks are only soft in that they help to provide that much sought after soft, flabby look.

Low Calorie Diet Drinks

Because of our weight problems, Americans are calorie conscious. As we attempt to get slim or stay slim we count and weigh almost everything we eat and drink, displaying an almost fanatical concern for the lowest caloried items possible. However, loss of calories is matched by loss of energy.

Envision the typical housewife trying to shed that surplus poundage by keeping her calorie intake very low. She may lose the undesired weight but more than likely she will likewise lose vital energy. Selecting items based on lowest calories, she may overlook the *quality* of these calories. She must never forget that her body constantly needs to be fed high quality food, especially when she is losing weight.

In counting calories, our weight-conscious friend eliminates soft drinks from her diet because they are so high in calories. Fruit and vegetable juices would serve as ideal substitutes but they contain as many calories as soft drinks and are also very high in carbohydrates. Carbohydrates! Just the mention of this food factor strikes terror within the overworked hearts of fat-riddled Americans. Why? Because unused carbohydrates will be stored in the body as fat. So we are instructed to avoid foods high in carbohydrates.

Once again modern technology has sensed our dilemma and created a product to solve the problem of a much needed low calorie, good tasting liquid. Enter DIET DRINKS, ready equipped, not with sugar high in calories and carbohydrates, but with artificial, low-calorie sweetness.

Advertising assures us of the value of these chemical drinks. We view the "beautiful people" enjoying the popular diet drinks. Slim and alluring females tell us that this drink helps keep them so attractive. Of course, most of the models in these ads must starve themselves to stay that slim and are not what one would call healthy. Thus commercials showing girls with big busts and small waists—gifts of youth and fortunate parentage—are not honest recommendations for any drink.

Let's step inside a bottle of your favorite diet drink. Remember, we are looking for food to nourish our bodies. Chemicals and artificiality of any kind fail the test.

We first encounter carbonated water, our friend from soft drinks. Diet drinks also contain the caffeine that makes coffee and soft drinks addicting and over-stimulating to the pancreas. Good reasons to be one of the switched generation.

Instead of sugar we discover an artificial sweetener. The most popular ones are saccharin and sorbitol, though for many years cyclamates were also used. Finally, after 20 years of harassment and volumes of irrefutable evidence from biochemists and research scientists, cyclamates were deemed a health hazard and removed from the market.

Saccharin, as I said earlier, has been used since the Food and Drug Administration became the food conscience of the United States. The founder of the FDA had access to extensive studies on the negative aspects —and they are all negative except for the economical aspect—of saccharin consumption. Saccharin is manufactured from toluene, a coal tar substance also used in making dyes and explosives. Scientists, not health fanatics, have proven that coal tar products can cause cancer.

And since it is artificial, not occurring naturally in foods, it possesses not one food value. It is truly a *non-food*.

Saccharin is 300 to 500 times sweeter than sugar. This is fantastic. Here is a chemical that contains none of the vitamins, minerals or enzymes found in the natural sugars of fruit and vegetable juices, but it possesses the stimulating effects equal to 300 to 500 times the same amount of food sugar. Just imagine the confusion inside your body. Here comes something that tastes like a food sugar, though many times sweeter, but it doesn't *feed you*.

I have never been able to understand how learned doctors could prescribe or suggest to their diabetic patients that they use saccharin as a sweetener. The diabetic is the last person in the world who can handle food sugar very well, much less a chemical substitute which will produce a much greater and more harmful effect. He needs the best nutrition possible, not a sickly, chemical substitute. Don't physicians know about the effects of saccharin?

The other popular artificial sweetener is sorbitol. When you read the label on a diet drink, if you can find it, you will learn that"sorbitol is a non-nutritive sweetener, metabolized as a carbohydrate but more slowly." What does this mean?

A non-nutritive sweetener is something that offers no food value. It supplies nothing with which to feed the body. Since it is a *non-food*, sorbitol clogs up the body with its chemical presence, and it is metabolized or broken down much slower than food carbohydrates. In other words, we face the problem of the body having to work harder and longer to eliminate this *non-food* than it would with the natural sugar in food. The longer it stays in the body, the greater the chance of chemical contamination. I hope you can understand that it is never wise to replace a food like fruit juice or milk with a chemical liquid mimicking the properties of a sweet food liquid but possessing none of its valuable food qualities.

Many dieters use diet drinks exclusively—with meals, between meals, in place of meals, or whenever they are thirsty. They think they can drink all they want because 12 ounces contains one or two or ten calories. If you drink these diet drinks, you are wasting stomach space just as you do in drinking coffee. Remember, the ingredients on the label are the ingredients that will soon fill your insides.

Drinking diet drinks with your meals neutralizes to a great extent the digestive capabilities of your stomach and will help you waste your food. Taste buds can be fooled, but cells cannot. On the other hand, *fruit juices like milk have "something for everybody."*

Alcohol—Vitamin Robber

In our discussion of *non-foods*, I am presenting different products that are commonly found in the standard diet. I include these products because they have no value in feeding the body but often substitute for nutritious food. It is especially important to count the quality of what you are eating when you are trying to shed those extra pounds. Trying to maintain a polite introduction to this last *non-food*, we will consider it purely from a food versus *non-food* viewpoint, overlooking the more obvious problems of chemical and emotional addiction.

It is very interesting and distressing to discover how much alcohol is annually consumed in the United States alone. Television, radio, and billboard commercials prate about all kinds of alcoholic beverages and how they should fit into our modern diet. The campaign must be effective, for everywhere we go wine or beer or hard liquor is served with meals, used at housewarming parties, and introduced before or after any worthwhile activity.

"Wine is good for digestion"; "A little shot of whiskey is good for your heart." The advertising overwhelms us in its announcement of the so-called positive effects of alcoholic consumption. Very seldom, except when presenting the problem of alcoholism, does one hear anything negative about alcohol. Well, settle back, you are going to hear why alcohol is a *non-food* and why it should be stricken from your diet.

Alcohol—every kind of alcohol—contains a large amount of carbohydrates but lacks B-vitamins. Your system must have B-vitamins with carbohydrates so that the carbohydrates can be digested. If B-vitamins do not accompany the carbohydrates, your body must provide them from its storehouse. Therefore, like refined sugar, alcohol robs the body of its precious stores of B-vitamins, which would break up the carbohydrates in alcohol and then eliminate them.

Alcohol does not feed the body. Even though certain nutritious foods are used to make alcohol, the final consumed product will not nourish the body. You get a little fuel, but that's all. The alcohol imbiber would profit much more by eating the raw ingredients. Alcohol will deliver a certain increase in energy but this is primarily created by the overacting of the pancreas. In the loose sense of the word, we should class alcohol as a refined sugar.

Alcohol, not eliminated through urination or perspiration, is stored as body fat. Cirrhosis of the liver, a condition of fatty deposits in and around the liver, is much higher in alcohol consumers than non-drinkers. The liver performs over 1000 different functions in the body. For instance, the liver is the filter system for the body, the producer of bile for the gall bladder's digestion of fats and fat soluble vitamins, the source of the hormonal material for the endocrine system, and the richest storehouse of protein, vitamins, minerals, and enzymes. Next to the heart, the liver is probably the most important organ in your body.

I am not saying that everyone who drinks wine or a favorite beer will end up with cirrhosis of the liver, but alcohol is not something that should remain as even an occasional entree in your diet.

Jim went to the doctor feeling tired and listless. It seemed all the fun had gone out of his life. Each day was a new battle with depression. His ailment was diagnosed as hypoglycemia and he was put on the standard hypoglycemic diet. Jim began to improve but he still had radical ups and downs in his blood sugar level. It was not until he eliminated the lunch martinis and dinner drinks that, in his own words, "he really began to live."

No matter what she did, Carmen could not lose that last five pounds that would put her back down to her high school weight. She would faithfully stay on her diet during the week but fail on the weekend. She would not get drunk but she would drink Friday night, Saturday night and sometimes Sunday. She drank, she said, just to be sociable. But she was not being very sociable to her body. When she stopped drinking her weight went down.

Sam had high blood pressure. It was common for industrial salesmen to have this ailment, his doctor told him. A change in diet and an exercise program lowered his blood pressure but it was still dangerously high. When Sam and I talked in a health food store, he told me all that he had done to get his blood pressure down. He told me everything, that is, except his alcohol consumption. After much evasion he confessed that he had three or four drinks a day. It was expected, he said, when he took a prospective client out. At night he had a couple of drinks to "unwind." I explained to him that as he was unwinding, his blood pressure was going up—alcohol causes blood vessels to constrict—thereby raising his blood pressure. He just couldn't believe this could be his problem but he agreed to cut down. He reduced his alcohol intake to one drink a day and sometimes none at all. Within a month his blood pressure was in the normal range.

Most people are reluctant to dispense with their glass of wine for dinner or their party cocktail or their winddown drink. After all, they don't drink that much alcohol. Oh no? Even if you enjoy only four drinks a week, that is a substantial amount of alcohol when considered over a 25-year period. Your body has to work hard to eliminate this *non-food*.

Alcohol is not good for digestion. In fact, since alcohol destroys B-vitamins, digestion will be hindered, not helped. The protein in your food may not be properly utilized because as the B-vitamins are washed away, so are a good many other digestive elements. This dilution of the digestive process may not show itself immediately in the form of some major illness but a less than optimum digestion promises a less than excellent state of health.

Most people I know class themselves as social drinkers, whatever that means. I often explain to them that it takes almost a week to completely eliminate the poisonous residue of alcohol from the body. Yes, I said "poisonous" because it is. You see, if alcohol does not feed the body, it must destroy it—and it does, cell by cell. Because the effects of alcohol are cumulative, they may not express themselves for many years, and then only indirectly.

Alcohol races the heart muscle, causing it to work harder and wear out faster. Coupled with the raising of blood cholesterol, alcohol presents a two-pronged attack on the heart and provides us with two more good reasons to strike it from our eating habits.

Drinking alcohol replaces food nourishment with *non-food* pollution. Our modern emphasis on ecology and environmental pollution should make us keenly aware of clogging our bodies with chemicals and other *non-food* products that are pleasing to the taste but repugnant to the body. Alcohol should be replaced by milk or fruit juice or vegetable juice. If you must drink any alcohol while employing this new way of eating, the only time to do it is eight hours after eating or eight hours before the next meal.

Notes

1. J.I. Rodale, *Encyclopedia of Common Diseases* (Emmaus, Penn.: Rodale Press, Inc., 1971) p. 145.

chapter five
The Staff of Life

"Man does not live by bread alone," but not many live without any! Whether we consume grains in cereals or toast, we eat a lot of it. Bread is a near-permanent part of everybody's diet. Yet we consistently make terrible choices in the kinds of bread we eat. Taste and color seem to determine which loaf graces our table.

If bread is to be the staff of life, we need to be sure we are not getting stuffed with products whose only benefit is increasing the profits of the bakers.

Bread for Life

You can look high and low, east and west, but nowhere will you find white grain. It simply does not exist. White flour and white bread are made from wheat, which contains vitamins, minerals, protein, carbohydrates, and other food factors. These elements make whole wheat a valuable food, but white bread has had all of these life-giving nutrients stripped from it.

White bread has a longer shelf life than wheat bread. Since everything seems to be geared toward preserving our food as long as possible, and since the *live* elements in food give it a short life expectancy, manufacturers remove the live element in wheat to fabricate white flour and white bread. Then they add chemical preservatives and the shelf life increases tremendously, thus creating more profit for the merchant and producer. Interestingly enough, when a rat is given a choice between white and wheat bread, he always goes for the wheat. Animals, unlike man, eat things that are good for them and are not easily fooled by taste.

Wheat germ and the wheat germ oil found in the embryo of the wheat kernel are two of the most important parts of wheat. These foods must be processed out before it is subjected to the rollers, pressers, bleaching agents and other chemical and manufacturing processes. For years wheat germ oil was a messy waste product. Only later did the manufacturers of white flour products discover that this oil contained a most valuable element, vitamin E. An entire financial empire was founded on one of the natural ingredients stripped from wheat during the production of white flour. So when you are shopping at your grocery store or health food store, delete those products that contain white bread, white flour or enriched flour. Enriched flour is that which has been enriched with chemical vitamins and minerals that were extracted in the processing of wheat to white in the first place. Whole wheat or any other whole grain does not need enriching because all the nutrients are still in the food.

The Popular Breakfast Cereals

The most popular advertising item geared for the younger television audiences is the breakfast cereal. Everytime we look around a new one is on the market shelf. Inside or on the colorful box, usually adorned by a popular cartoon character or a healthy athlete, we discover a prize—no, not the cereal but the game or toy we get as a bonus when we buy the cereal. We would be better off dumping out the cereal and keeping the prize.

Before buying your favorite breakfast cereal, read the ingredients label on the panel—if you can find it amidst the bright colors, games and ridiculous claims. Although package appearance is very important in selling products, we do not eat the container. We should purchase products according to their content and not because of their fancy packaging. What is inside our pretty-packaged cereals? White flour, of course. But what else?

Almost all breakfast cereals contain some form of refined sugar. A good deal of sugar, sometimes as much as 50 percent, must be added to make the taste of refined grains palatable. Oh yes, because the food processors are thinking of our health they add chemical vitamins to the cereal to replace the ones they processed out.

Now comes the most hideous element. With almost no exceptions our breakfast cereals contain some kind of preservatives to keep them fresher longer. The most widely used preservatives are BHA and BHT *(butylated hydroxyanisole* and *butylated hydroxytoluene)* the same chemicals used in embalming fluids. While these chemicals may be very good for embalming the dead body, I don't recommend them for a live one. Read the cereal labels and pass by any cereals that contain refined sugar, chemical vitamins, white flour, BHA and BHT. Don't be misled by "natural cereals." Stick to the whole grain cereals and get the *whole food.*

chapter six

Satisfying Your Sweet Tooth

From the neighborhood ice cream truck to fancy restaurants, every attempt is being made to satisfy our sweet tooth. All kinds of treats delight and tempt us and beg our consumption. There is really nothing wrong with "sweets" as long as they are food sweets. The important thing is to know what belongs inside your body and what, for health's sake, should never enter.

I Scream for Ice Cream

No Sunday supper or family dinner is complete without at least one dish of ice cream, a wholesome food topping off a good meal. Surprise, surprise! To be called ice cream the product need contain only 20 percent of any dairy product like cream, milk, or eggs. The rest is up to the imaginative mind of the food chemist. You would do well to read a number of authoritative books on ice cream manufacturing, but let us look at a couple of interesting facts.

Commercial ice cream is not made from cream or eggs, for these ingredients are too expensive. Certain chemicals can be joined together to mimic effectively the taste and texture of cream and eggs. Unfortunately, chemicals may taste like food, but they do not feed the body.

Nowadays, ice cream comes in a variety of flavors. When you visit an ice cream parlor, it takes more time to read the menu than to get your dish or cone. Raspberry, vanilla, chocolate, strawberry ... any flavor your heart desires. But in buying this ice cream, you don't always get raspberries or strawberries, but chemicals made up to represent and taste like the natural flavors that appeared on the menu. And, again, the sweetener in the ice cream comes from our old friend, refined sugar—as much as four tablespoons per serving. Another nutritional disaster.

To capture a vivid picture of the kinds of chemicals used in ice cream, I have lifted a section on ice cream flavors out of *Our Poisoned Earth and Sky* published by Rodale Press, whom I consider the best and most reliable source for nutritional information.

"Commercial ice creams almost never use the natural substance to attain the bulk of the flavor intended. In the book *Food Flavorings* by Merory, we came across a chapter entitled Imitation Flavors. Many of these formulas are the ones to flavor the ice cream we are offered. Here is the recipe for banana flavorings:

7.2 grams imitation violet-formula mf 140
22.0 grams benzyl propionate
24.0 grams ethyl caproate
24.0 grams heliotropin

24.0 grams vanillin
24.0 grams coumarin substitute
40.0 grams linalool
60.0 grams amyl valerate
120.0 grams amyl butyrate
120.0 grams acetaldehyde
534.8 grams amyl acetate

We have investigated these ingredients in the Merck Index and came up with some surprising and disconcerting background on some of those that were listed. Heliotropin was found to be a drug which, if used in large amounts, will cause depression of the central nervous system. Amyl valerate is a substance that has been used as a sedative for hysteria. Amyl acetate is used to perfume shoe polish and in the manufacture of artificial silk, leather and in dyeing and finishing textiles. It is also known to cause headache, fatigue, and irritation of mucous membranes from continuous exposure. Acetaldehyde is used, among other things, in the manufacturing of plastics. It irritates the mucous membranes, and has a general narcotic action. Large doses may cause death through respiratory paralysis. Its toxicity symptoms are similar to those of chronic paralysis.

Other flavorings containing specific undesirable ingredients are: cherry piperonal, substance used to kill lice; aldehyde C-17, an inflammable liquid used in aniline dyes, plastics and synthetic rubber; pineapple-ethyl acetate, a chemical used for cleaning textiles, whose vapors may be irritating to the mucous membranes, and may damage the heart, the kidneys, and the liver; nut flavor-butyaldehyde, used in rubber cement, rubber accelerators, and synthetic resins; strawberry-benzyl acetate, a substance that can cause vomiting and diarrhea; black walnut-ammonium valerate, a medical sedative."[1]

There is, however, a good tasting, healthy replacement for commercial *non-food* ice cream: *honey ice cream*, made from honey, cream, eggs, and the real fruit, not the chemical flavors. A couple of brands on the market advertise themselves as natural ice creams, but don't be fooled by nice-sounding commercials or healthy claims. *Read the label.* Don't buy if it includes refined sugar, for sugar is a robber, not a feeder. In fact imitation ice creams contain almost 70 percent refined sugar. This is certainly not my idea of a "natural" ice cream.

Chocolate: Let It Melt in Your Hands, Not in Your Body

South America supplies us with the brown gold. The cocoa bean gives us the chocolate covering for our candies, our cakes, our M&Ms, and anything else in need of a rich, dark color. Chocolate, of course, is the kissing cousin of refined sugar. They are usually found together. When the candy companies make chocolate or milk chocolate, sugar is normally one of the added ingredients. Because chocolate by nature is bitter, the refined sugar is necessary for the candy palate. Since chocolate supplies no vitamins, minerals or enzymes, it is another *non-food*.

Besides containing refined sugar, chocolate deserves a place on our *non-food* list for other reasons. For instance, it contains *theobromine*, a substance that is so closely related to caffeine and produces the same reaction as caffeine that we can consider it caffeine. It destroys vitamins, overactivates the pancreas, upsets the nervous system, dilutes the stomach juices, and generally distorts the metabolic processes in the body.[2]

Chocolate also contains oxalic acid, a compound that combines with the calcium in the body and renders the calcium unusable. This calcium oxalate, the new compound of calcium and oxalic acid, is the chief component of kidney stones. Any connection? Quit eating chocolate and don't find out.[3]

Most people eat candy because it gives them a lift. And well it should. Chocolate and refined sugar are two of the highest calorie sources available. However, since they don't contain any carbohydrate digesting B-vitamins, the body must rob itself of these perishable vitamins. Make other choices for quick energy that don't steal from your body.

Here is still another shocker. Recently chocolate has been found to contain traces of *cocaine*. Is this something you should be eating? Not if you want to feed your body.

Chocolate Substitute—Carob

Carob is the natural food substitute for chocolate. It grows on the carob trees in pods. Carob pods are crushed and ground into a brown powder that has the same basic texture and color as chocolate. Carob contains B-vitamins, protein, minerals and other food nutrients. It contains no caffeine, and you need no sugar to cover a bitter taste, for carob is naturally sweet.

There is really nothing wrong with eating candy bars. You must, however, eat food bars, not junk bars. As you read the fine, almost invisible print on the candy bar wrapper, look for our enemies, chocolate and refined sugar. Health food stores and many regular grocery stores now carry a variety of "healthy candy." But beware! Buying something in a health food store or a health food section is no automatic guarantee that a product does not contain chocolate or refined sugar. Dextrose, sucrose, lactose, maltose, fructose, glucose, corn syrup, corn starch and raisin syrup are just a few of the pseudonyms refined sugar uses. Fructose, for instance, a fruit sugar and a food when found in fruit along with its needed companions, becomes a *non-food* when it is extracted from fruit to be used as a sweetener. Fructose is a refined sugar because the vitamins, minerals and other nutrients have been processed away leaving only the sugar.

Here is another word to the wise concerning those products that read "naturally sweetened" or "contains artificial sweetener." To a chemist, sugar, refined or otherwise, is a "natural sweetener." Unless the label specifically says otherwise, you can count on some sort of refined sugar being used as the sweetening agent. "No sugar added" does not mean the same as "this product contains no sugar," for sugar may have been used earlier in the manufacturing process. You must check those labels very closely.

Honey is the obvious alternative for candy bar sweetener, for it contains all the factors missing in refined sugar. Since we are setting up a program to feed the body as well as possible, I would certainly stay away from sugar sweetened candy and buy only those treats that contain honey.

There are many food bars on the market now that either are not cooked or are cooked very little and need no sweetener. The fruits, seeds, or nuts supply the sweet taste. These are foods that will give you needed energy if you start to drag in the afternoon or if you miss a meal.

One more word of caution. All carob-coated bars contain sugar. I repeat: *all carob-coated bars contain sugar.* For years the public was not informed of this. In fact, for a long time I recommended carob-coated bars to diabetics because the bar contained no sugar. Unfortunately, that was a half-truth. The bar did not contain sugar, but the *coating* did.

Candy bar makers report that they are forced to use

sugar in carob-coated bars because honey when heated, as the candy concoction demands, gets gummy and sticky. This messes up the vats and all other equipment used in making the carob-coated bar. I am sure this is true, but I am equally certain that if they tried harder they could find a way to use honey. At any rate, until a significant change occurs, do not eat carob-coated bars.

For someone who enjoys chocolate in his milk, I would suggest carob powder, the ground-up powder of carob pods. However, if you have been hooked on chocolate for some time, you may not find carob sweet enough for you, so I suggest that you add a little honey at first. Soon you will find that the honey is no longer required. Beware of the *carob drink powders*. They help sweeten your carob by adding refined sugar. *Read those labels.*

Notes

1. J.I. Rodale, *Our Poisoned Earth and Sky* (Emmaus, Penn.: Rodale Press, Inc., 1964).
2. J.I. Rodale, *Health Builders* (Emmaus, Penn.: Rodale Press, Inc., 1957), p. 207.
3. Ibid.

chapter seven

Smoke Gets in Your Eyes— and Everywhere Else

So much has been written on the dangers of smoking that every reader must acknowledge that this habit is far from healthy. You smokers are aware of the dangers you are taking when you light up. Some effects, however, are not heavily advertised.

Nicotine raises the blood cholesterol level. In some way the nicotine causes many of the unsaturated fats circulating in the blood stream to become saturated and settle in the arterial walls and the lining of the veins.

Nicotine is a powerfully addicting drug. Many people who want to quit smoking but cannot are victims of this powerful substance. You can switch to less tar and nicotine cigarettes but, as long as you smoke any nicotine, you are controlled. More people are hooked on cigarettes than all illegal drugs combined.

Smoking is very irritating to the mucous membranes in the mouth, nose, throat, lungs and digestive tract. Smoking will actually dry up these naturally moist areas that help in fighting bacteria invaders and hinder avenues for cell growth, repair, and normal healthy cell life. Consequently, smokers are more susceptible to colds, general infections and respiratory illnesses. If the mucous membranes could stay moist, the resistance would remain much higher.

Smoking affects the nervous system. The smoke you inhale may seem to produce an immediate calming effect on your nerves, but this is just a facade. Upon the inhalation of smoke, your B-vitamins, which are most important for a calm nervous system, are dispatched to help rid the body of this dangerous poison. In addition to their many other attributes, B-vitamins are antitoxins. One of the storehouses for this group of vitamins is the nervous system, so you are robbing your nervous system of these necessary nutrients so vital for nerve impulses and energy transfer. The myelin sheath, the covering of the nerve endings, must contain certain enzymes to allow nerves to relax properly. When the B-vitamins are used for waste removal instead of nerve nourishment, you develop an unhealthy, jumpy nervous system.

Smoking distorts a normal appetite. Have you ever noticed the number of converted smokers who complain of gaining weight after they quit smoking? Well, there are a couple of good reasons for this. A smoker overactivates his nervous system, creates a shortage of B-vitamins, falsely prepares the body for the digestion of food and, most important of all, numbs the delicate appetite control found in the brain. When he no longer smokes, his body reacts by seeking more than normal requirements of food to repair the damage done by the smoking and to feed starving cells. If he does gain weight at first, he should not be alarmed. His body is seeking and finally receiving the nutrients it needs to stay healthy.

Smokers who are overweight suffer the same consequences but react in a different way. They are likewise starving. But instead of eating normally, they overeat and store the extra as fat. The difference lies in the individual response to a depleted, overactive nervous system. In both cases, the normal appetite is perverted by smoking. Thus Mr. Smoker eats too much or too little.

John came to the health spa to shed 30 pounds he didn't need and do something about the "wind" he'd lost. He was a successful stockbroker and his only physical activity was the basketball he played two nights a week. John knew all the reasons why he shouldn't smoke, and he knew what a risk he was taking. However, he didn't let the facts confuse him until he noticed he wasn't as fast as he once was and his endurance was decreasing. He chalked these problems up to being overweight and set about getting back to his high school weight of 15 years before. He "cut down" from two packs of cigarettes a day to one pack. However, he found that as he exercised in the spa, his appetite increased. He gained 10 more pounds and he was more tired than before.

It took three months to convince John that his real problem was smoking. A radical change in eating habits and a complete abstinence from cigarettes soon helped him lose 33 pounds and increased his stamina and endurance. His appetite also changed. Although he was exercising harder than ever and eating more food than when he was smoking, he lost weight and kept it off.

He no longer had a craving for sweets and snacks.

Often smokers will be truly malnourished because cigarettes are destroying many vital nutrients, upsetting proper digestion and increasing their appetites to supply more food to feed their smoke-filled bodies.

Smoking forces the blood vessels to constrict, thereby causing the openings in the veins and arteries to become smaller. The requirement for blood remains the same but the passages are now smaller. This can easily be compared to what happens when there is construction on a busy highway. When traffic is constant, even with all lanes open, our automobiles at times crawl along bumper to bumper. But if one or more lanes close due to road work, the remaining lane or lanes become terribly congested and progress is measured in minutes, not miles. Likewise when blood vessels shrink in size, the heart must work much harder to push needed nutrients to the different parts of the body.

These highways of blood can suffer roadblocks and accordingly park their valuable cargo alongside the vessel walls like a car that has overheated or run out of gas. We all suffer with obstructions in our blood vessels to some degree, but if you smoke you increase the danger to your circulation. Poor circulation prohibits proper materials from getting to the intended cells. Also cell waste products will be poorly removed. Toxemia is one result of this inefficient waste removal.[1]

Carbon monoxide in cigarette smoke displaces oxygen in the blood system. Carbon monoxide is unavoidably sucked into the body with the smoke. It seeks out and uses up the oxygen transported by the red cells, displacing the oxygen at an alarming rate. Oxygen is so very important because it functions as the fire for the burning of food in the cells. Thus anyone low on oxygen has very poor food assimilation.

I know of no safe substitute for tobacco. No matter

what you smoke, it is still dangerous to your body because you inject poisonous tars and gases into your body. And its deadliness is heightened when you are trying to change your metabolism and lose weight. The process of withdrawal is bad now, but it is much worse later on. Your food will even taste better when you stop "curing" it in your *smokehouse.*

Notes

1. J.H. Tilden, *Toxemia: The Basic Causes of Disease* (Chicago: Natural Hygiene Press, 1974).

part three

A Healthy Approach to Weight Loss

chapter eight

Where Others Have Gone Before

In the first part of this book we dealt, unfortunately but necessarily, with what not to eat and why. You should now be more aware that our food is not what it should be. *Reading labels* is necessary for survival. Buying a product because it is a name brand, without checking the ingredients panel, is committing nutritional suicide.

Although we have not mentioned this lately, the title of this book is *How to Be Fit and Free.* Free from what? Obviously free from being overweight but also free from misinformation concerning what is good to eat and what is not. You further need to be free of wild claims for weight-loss gimmicks and modern "scientifically proven diets." A medical degree or laboratory endorsement does not guarantee a healthy approach to weight loss.

And that should be our primary concern: *A healthy approach to weight loss.*

There are numerous ways of losing weight, many of which are illogical and some that are downright dangerous. One woman, for instance, lost 30 pounds in a month by drinking diet drinks. She lost the weight so she must have had a good diet, right? Wrong! The ends do not justify the means. To illustrate my point, let's see where others in the weight-loss game have gone before.

Calorie Counting

The most popular approach to weight loss involves calorie counting. In fact, many diets ask you to count calories in conjunction with their own special program. Their attention, however, is focused entirely on the quantity of calories, not on the quality of those calories.

Sue taught high school home economics. Her special interest was nutrition. She had a very strong academic background in foods and diets. Yet for all her knowledge she could not solve the recurring weight problem she suffered. A tiny girl, five-feet-two-inches, her weight kept creeping up beyond 120 pounds. The only way she could lose weight was to count calories. She would lose 10 to 15 pounds and then gain it back again. In a five-year period she must have gained and lost over 100 pounds. Sometimes uncontrollable desires for certain foods would push her weight up again; other times she ate too much because she was bored. When the weight came back, in just a short time, she was once again counting calories.

A calorie is a unit of energy. If you consume more calories than you use up, you put on weight. Conversely, if you utilize more calories than you consume, you will lose weight. So with a minimum of logic you can see that if you want to lose weight you simply cut down on your calories. The calories go down and the fat peels off.

Suddenly we are confronted with a major dilemma. The body needs to be fed food—good food—all the time, especially when you are trying to lose weight. The organs and muscles do not recognize your desire to be thinner. They just want to be fed. They perform nonstop 24 hours a day and consequently need 24-hour-a-day nutrition. Choosing low calorie *non-food* products may help to achieve your weight goal but they certainly do not feed your body.

An interesting and distressing fact about calorie counters is that they invariably gain the weight back. Why? Because they can't stay on their low-calorie diets for very long. First they experience a great loss of energy. In this tired state, they continue on their low-calorie diets through sheer mental energy and drive. But their brains, that can drive them when they have no energy and when their bodies are pleading for rest or more food, eventually get tired too. Remember, the brain, which is only one-fiftieth of the total weight of the body, uses over 50 percent of the total food we consume to keep it running properly. When the brain finally gets underfed, the dieter is really in trouble.

Calorie counters gain their weight back because their bodies are underfed during the dieting process. They think only of the fat they wish to lose, not the body they must maintain. It is not possible to count calories alone and expect to keep your weight down, for other factors are involved. An unbalanced diet founded on quantity of calories consumed rather than quality of calories is doomed to failure. You may realize temporary weight change, but you soon go back to eating the way you did before. Look for a diet you can use the rest of your life. Be conscious of what you are eating and *what that food will do for you or to you.*

Starvation Diets

If you watch any television at all, you have encountered the clothing industry's idea of the attractive woman: Miss Super-Skinny. She must stay that way to wear the latest high fashions. Her face is bony and her eyes often appear sunken.

One year, while working for Jack LaLanne, I had the opportunity to observe a few fashion models as I provided nutritional guidance at a health spa that was frequented by a number of people in the movie and television industry. Without exception, the girls I met literally had to starve themselves to maintain their slight weight and keep their modeling careers. *Skinny they were; healthy they weren't.* Barely living on enough to feed a gnat and deriving their energy from a variety of pills, they were wasting their health and youth potential.

The preceding is an extreme example, but many overweight women and men adopt starvation diets to lose that last 10 or 15 pounds. This is one of the worst things they can do.

One well-known TV and movie personality keeps her slim appearance by starving herself. Between acting jobs she may gain 15 to 20 pounds. So, when she is in some kind of production she eats next to nothing to get her weight back down. Living on pills and nerves she "slims in," as she calls it. She is a bundle of nerves and only a fantastically strong will keeps her from drowning in tears over the miseries she suffers to "be beautiful."

The last few years, however, her face and body have not so easily responded to her starvation diet and she is finding it harder to keep her weight down and the wrinkles off. It is amazing to me how attractive she still is, considering the abuse she gives her body.

Someone who is overweight has probably tried many diets which never do the job. However, he knows one plan that always works: *Stop eating.* "I know that when I stop eating or eat very little, my body will live off the extra fat I am carrying. Starve long enough and I will lose all I want." Nothing could be further from the truth.

In the first place, fat does not burn by itself; it requires protein to break down fatty tissue. During a starvation diet, since protein is not being supplied through food, the body must draw on its own *protein resources* in the organs and muscle tissues to burn the fat. The body seems to rob its protein bank first in the small muscles of the eyes and the face, which explains why so many men and women have that haggard, drained, washed-out look on their faces while enduring their starvation schedules.

If the dieter continues for very long, energy willing, his liver, kidneys and other organs will give up some of their protein reserves. Remember, these reserves are in the body for emergencies and for normal repair and rebuilding of the tissues. They are too valuable to be splurged as a source of energy. The person who keeps making withdrawals without depositing something, will soon be physically bankrupt.

When you finally go off your starvation diet after a week or so and start eating as you normally do, you will find all your weight back, plus some. This is because your body is attempting to reinstate a positive balance in the protein reserves that have been ravaged.

Starving always leads to death. Robbing protein reserves could create a problem if your body encountered a severe sickness or traumatic experience. Starvation diets will not promote health, insure a trim energetic body, or produce permanent results.

Fat Shots

A supposedly scientifically proven method of weight

loss may be labeled *fat shots.* Conducted under strict medical supervision, this program has worked successfully for thousands of people over the last 30 years. With four out of five people being overweight, as the ad says, this is the modern and easy way to shed that extra weight and improve your appearance, stamina, drive, attractiveness, and performance quickly and safely. This sounds just too good to be true. Can this be the great fat hope? What exactly is Dr. Simeon's method?

Fat shots are injections of a hormone found in the urine of pregnant women. This hormone supposedly affects the fat-burning rate of the body. In other words, this hormone, *gonadotrophin* (combined with the frozen food dinners also supplied by this diet program) will speed up the rate at which the body will burn up its own useless fat. The hormone program, according to the proponents of Dr. Simeon's procedure, is the safest and easiest way to lose weight quickly.

In the first place, it is a gimmick, a quick and easy way to Thindom. Taking some shots for a few weeks and visiting a man in a white coat seem like a small price to pay for losing excess weight. (By the way, it isn't cheap!) No habits to change, no hard regimens to follow. Just shoot the weight off. But beware of gimmicks! They sometimes cost more than you bargained for.

What kind of food do you eat? *Frozen food dinners!* You have to be kidding! After vitamins and minerals are processed out and chemical vitamins and *non-food* flavorings and preservatives are added, what is left in most commercial foods cannot be labeled food. To institute this as the main staple in a weight losing diet is really ridiculous. Even without the shots, the food would certainly be at the top of one's dietary "hate parade."

But how long does this weight stay off? Those who take the hormone shots realize some weight loss, but unfortunately, it inevitably comes back. What good is weight loss that is not permanent?

If the hormone affects the fat-burning capabilities of the body, what else does it influence? What does it do to the delicate hormonal balance of the body?

If this injection affects the delicate hormonal balance of the woman, what results may appear in the woman's body or that of her offspring? Did you know that hormone problems associated with taking hormone pills, birth control pills, or these gonadotrophin shots may not arise for 20 or 30 years?

There is a definite danger in taking hormones of any kind. I have known several weight lifters who have suffered tumors, the loss of one testicle, liver malfunctions, and a drastic decrease in their sex drives. Two men, for six months, had no sex drive whatsoever. All these symptoms occurred during or shortly after taking hormones.

I know of no one who will come right out and say that hormones will cause this or that problem. But researchers and some scientists say that hormones *could* cause problems. Many researchers are now saying that there could be a danger for women who take estrogen.

Even if fat shots only affected a small percentage, I certainly would not want to be included in that group. Would you? Losing weight is much easier than that—and not so risky.

Apart from the fact that the treatment is centered on less than the best food selection and requires an injection of chemical hormones, this fantastic scientific discovery is nothing more than an expensive, dishonest gimmick. Supervision by medical doctors and nurses in medical clinics may lend professionalism to the treatment and give confidence to their patients, but it does not disguise the fact that it is a gimmick. Advertisements applaud the fact that the patient need not struggle with exercise or hard-to-stay-on diets. They forget to mention, however, that all that easily discarded weight will return in triumph.

A weight reduction program should be judged positively or negatively on its ability to keep the weight off permanently and in no way cause injury. *Stay away from commercial gimmicks.* It didn't take shots to create the overweight condition and it is not necessary to take shots to correct it.

High Protein-Low Carbohydrate Diets

Now we come to another popular reducing diet. This diet is not new at all. In fact, the high protein-low carbohydrate diet has been used by many people, though they may have been unaware of it. A number of my weight-lifting friends have resorted to it to keep their weight down in order to stay in a weight class. Yet the high amount of protein allows them to work out hard, keep their strength up, and maintain a high protein reserve to call upon in a stress situation like a contest.

Physique contestants, almost to a man, have employed some form of this diet in preparing for a physique contest. The high amount of protein enables them to keep their energy level high as they lose that 10 to 30 pounds for the next contest. Their razor-sharp muscular appearance is more easily attained when they eliminate carbohydrates. At the same time, because of the exclusiveness of the protein diet, they can reduce their waists and still maintain muscle size on other parts of their body.

As a matter of fact, most athletes from time to time have found this diet, often by instinct alone, an effective method of getting to their particular weight requirements for competition in their sport. They may not be aware of the technical aspects of the diet, but they are firsthand observers of the results. Somewhere along the line a doctor or some quick-talking salesman appropriated the diet and gave it a fancy name, assuming credit for its origin. I only mention this to illustrate that the high protein-low carbohydrate diet is not a new way to lose weight. But what are the principles behind this diet?

Carbohydrates, the cheapest form of fuel for the body, are the main offenders in adding fat. One who consumes a high amount of carbohydrates and engages in little physical activity will surely gain weight. As a rule, most people include far too many carbohydrate-rich foods in their daily eating patterns. As you remember when we discussed refined sugar, as much as 60 percent of regular grocery foods have some kind of refined sweetener in them. The more you eat, the more you want. Since we take in too many carbohydrates, it makes sense to cut down on them.

Protein is required by every cell in the body. It repairs broken tissues and supplies the raw materials to replace old cells with new ones. Protein, however, does one very important task as far as the overweight person is concerned: it burns or breaks down fat. Increase your protein intake and increase your fat burning. It is true, as the pushers of this plan testify, that we don't need all those carbohydrates. Over 65 percent of all protein and 35 percent of all fat is converted into carbohydrates for energy.

A number of problems may arise in following this high protein-low carbohydrate diet. In the first place, this diet makes no distinction between food carbohydrates and non-food carbohydrates. Non-food carbohydrates should always be avoided whether one is trying to lose weight or not. They supply the form of fuel but no substance to feed the body.

It is not wise to eliminate all carbohydrates. They actually help assimilate the protein we eat. The body uses this food to get the machine moving. Total elimination of carbohydrates interferes with the complex digestive chain of events necessary to utilize protein. Oh, sure, you will still digest some of the protein and lose weight, but you will waste much of it.

"Wasteful" sums up the high protein-low carbohydrate diet. Protein is usually the most expensive food in your budget. To use this first class food for energy instead of using it to replace and build tissue is like putting premium gasoline in a low octane car. You will get the required energy but at a higher price than necessary. A certain amount of food carbohydrates will supply your body with necessary energy without drawing on the protein supply.

Women have a natural tendency toward a sweet tooth. I don't know why, but when they experience "emotional lows" they often run to sweet treats. Therefore, the very low carbohydrate diet will in a short time, depending on the particular needs of the individual, increase her sharp appetite for sweets. But craving such food indicates that her body is trying to communicate something important. In this case, she is not getting enough natural food carbohydrates. While her body is manufacturing some carbohydrates from the protein, it still needs good food sweets.

There must be something in carbohydrates that is lacking in other foods. Whatever it is, your body functions better when it is fed good food carbohydrates along with the other food elements. Cutting down on carbohydrates to the point of total or nearly total abstinence may very well increase irritability and lessen your ability to stay on the diet.

Because the high protein diet relies on a single food

element, it is terribly unbalanced. Fats, carbohydrates, minerals, fruits and vegetables are too important food factors to neglect. Because food factors work together to properly feed the body, an overweight body should not be deprived of any necessary nutrients. Fat cells, like all other body cells, are living and need constant nourishment. To lose the fat, you must first feed it.

The last and best reason to reject the high protein-low carbohydrate diet is that, when you climb off the diet, the weight climbs back on. Obviously, this is not true weight loss and you have bravely endured your diet torture in vain. In the long run a diet should be judged only by its ability to help you lose weight permanently. A diet so unbalanced, expensive and temporary is a bad choice for correction of weight problems.

Vegetables Only: No Meat for Me

As the health food craze settled into the accepted circles of the commercial business world, many health doctrines, philosophies and cults took shape and enlisted followers. One of these movements I call "vegetables only, please." The vegetarian health system follows a diet plan that eliminates all animal products. People adopt the vegetarian regimen for a variety of reasons, many of which we can learn from and incorporate into our eating life-style.

Meat products are heavily polluted by chemicals and other non-foods. Cattle, for instance, eat grass and grains that are chemically fertilized. Chemical fertilization robs the plants of natural minerals. In addition this cattle feed has been sprayed with pesticides, insecticides and herbicides. The residue of these poisons remains in the plant and then takes permanent residence in the animal that consumes them.

Cattle that eat poison-filled grains are then further

maligned by hormones that are added to their daily fare (such as diethylstilbestrol, DES), which helps to fatten them.

Cowboys used to run the herds hard in cattle drives for several days prior to reaching their destination. Then they let the cattle gorge themselves on water a short time before they reached the stockyards. The slaughtered steers left much of their weight on the slaughterhouse floors as excess fluid. In a similar way DES steers add weight through fat and water which is cooked out on the stove.

At this writing scientists have found that DES is a potential cancer-causing drug; thus DES injections are no longer allowed. However, because this hormone stimulates better utilization of food with much less waste, DES can be implanted in the cattle's ears. This way the cattleman can use the hormone without passing on dangerous residues to consumers. Residues, however, have been found in slaughtered cattle.

Incidentally, DES is the same hormone women have been taking in the form of oral contraceptives. There is much suspicion among several research groups that the high consumption of DES in meats is the main reason young girls are maturing sexually so much earlier than their mothers and grandmothers. DES seems to upset the delicate hormonal clock inside a woman.

Vegetarians, consequently, steer clear (pardon the pun) of meat because it is a very polluted food. More often than not, the meat in the grocery store has been pen fed in contrast to pasture fed. (The less cattle move around the less food they eat and the bigger the profit margin for fatter meat, much of which you cook out on your stove.)

Heavy meat consumption has been accused of producing excessive amounts of uric acid, the advance guard of gout and other joint problems. Eliminate meat and cut down on your chances of suffering the painful misery of uric acid crystals in shoulders and other joints.[1] Incomplete digestion of animal protein leaves behind tiny, milky-white crystals which irritate and inflame the soft mucous membranes in the joints. There are few pains as excruciating.

Vegetarians realize that raw fruits and vegetables are loaded with enzymes which help to assimilate all the food one consumes. We could all use a helping hand in getting more nutrients from the foods we eat. Eating some sort of raw vegetable or fruit with meals will supply the live enzymes that are most necessary to digest the protein, carbohydrates, and fats. These enzymes are easily destroyed by heat; so raw fruits and vegetables, if not the only source, are certainly the cheapest and most available. Frozen or cooked vegetables and fruits do not supply enzymes.

When vegetarians eliminate animal protein from their diets they do not ignore the need for protein in the human body. Instead, they gain their protein from nuts and seeds, such as sunflower and sesame seeds. Nuts and seeds do not form uric acid crystals. Unlike meat, they are easy to fix. Just put them in a dish and eat them raw.

Another vegetarian plus is the fantastic cleansing effect of raw fruits and vegetables on the body. As we observed earlier, "You are what you assimilate from what you eat." None of us completely digests the food we eat; in fact, many of us are regularly plagued by poor digestion. It may not manifest itself the way low resistance manifests itself in a cold or lingering infection but it is still with us. I feel strongly that this poor assimilation of foods is the *prima facie* cause for all degenerative diseases. Taking digestive tablets or digestive aids will not really correct the situation. Oh sure, the body will be getting some things it may be deficient in, but it will not heal itself. Let me explain by example.

If your body fails to produce enough hydrochloric acid to adequately digest protein and other foods and you supply the hydrochloric acid in the form of hydrochloric acid tablets, your body, seeking to do what is easiest, will rely on the tablets to perform the function it cannot. In such a context, the food may be digested better but meanwhile the digestion process is getting worse. You are using a nutritional crutch for digestion rather than feeding your body the necessary, and possibly missing, elements your body requires to correct digestive inadequacies on its own. Raw fruits and vegetables supply many elements that may be missing from your diet that can develop your digestive muscles.

If you don't use your food well, you will waste a little or much of it. This waste can then back up in the intestinal tract and cause many problems. Fruits and vegetables have a cleansing effect on this partly digested food matter. Left to its own devices, poorly digested food can cause constipation, irregularity and sluggishness, known as *lower abdominal bloat.* Many people who try to reduce their midsections would be surprised to know that often this extra weight is not all fatty tissue; some of it is bloat from poorly digested food which is literally rotting in their intestinal tract. Cellulose, the indigestible protein in raw vegetables, is the *Drano* for the large and small intestines. Cellulose has a churning, grinding way of breaking up bloat-producing matter. On the vegetarian diet you will probably see your waist get smaller without much loss of weight. This is because cellulose is stripping the intestinal tract.

As a program to promote weight loss and establish an eating program for the rest of your life the vegetarian diet has many advantages; however this diet program also has some weaknesses.

A dedicated vegetarian commonly states that meat was never intended to be eaten by man. In fact, he may insist that man does not really have the digestive capabilities to utilize animal protein. He may further discuss the similarities between man and his vegetarian, evolutionary cousin and predecessor, the ape. However, since man was created in God's image, a special creation (not a million-year happenstance or a scientifically unsubstantiated mutational process), this argument holds no water. In line with such a contention, the vegetarian may also bring to our attention that the ape who eats only vegetables and fruits still persists in being one of the most vigorous and healthiest animals in the jungle.

In the first place, the ape can manufacture his complete proteins from some incomplete protein sources—which is something we cannot do. The ape must possess some digestive aid we do not possess. Since God gave him the innate knowledge to know what he needs to stay healthy, a wild ape will eat what is good for him.

In the second place, our bodies are actually physically prepared to digest animal protein. Hydrochloric acid in the stomach is present for just this purpose. Carbohydrates and starches are digested to a large extent by the enzymes and digestive juices in the mouth, saliva, and the intestinal tract. Fats, nuts and vegetable-type proteins are mostly digested by the liver, gall bladder, and intestinal tract. Vegetable protein contains such complex and hard-to-break-down structures that they pass into the intestinal tract for further digestion.

As long as you don't dilute the stomach environment by *non-foods*, you will be able to digest animal protein quite nicely. And since animal protein is a complete protein source, containing all the essential amino acids, it guarantees you a quicker and more readily available source of protein for rebuilding tissue and meeting everyday body needs. Nuts, seeds, fruits and vegetables are very important, but animal protein is paramount because, curiously, it is most like our own body protein.

Unfortunately, in the vegetarian diet regimen many protein sources are incomplete. They don't contain some of the amino acids our bodies need and can't manufacture. Of the approximately 22 amino acids, the body can make all but eight. Without these eight essential amino acids, the body simply cannot assimilate that source of protein. The answer, of course, is to combine the incomplete proteins with complete proteins. For instance, if you eat a nut that does not have any of the essential amino acid threonine, but contains all the other essential acids, then you should eat a seed or a nut that includes the missing threonine. In this manner you will supply all the essential amino acids at one time. Remember, your body can only use the protein when all the essential amino acids are present at the same time.

Several of my acquaintances are vegetarians who successfully combine their protein sources. However, I don't live to eat, I eat to live, and I think most of us would find it boring, impractical, and too time consuming to practice the art of food combining for every meal. And besides, there must be some problem with a diet program that is so notoriously lacking in the essential amino acids that one must constantly watch his notebook and protein chart. Animal proteins, however are all complete proteins, with all the essential amino acids.

In addition, vegetarian diets lack one of the most vital elements a human must have—B-12.[2] Vitamin B-12 is essential for the formation of red blood cells in bone marrow. Without B-12 fatigue sets in. B-12 is necessary for the manufacture of good red blood to carry oxygen to all the cells. Do without this element for any length of time and you are asking for trouble. Anemia could be right around the corner. There is no B-12 in vegetable sources outside of what little exists in the fuzz of comfrey leaves. Liver is the richest source of this vitamin. Many vegetarians—intelligent ones, I might add—realize the problem and supplement their diet with B-12 tablets. However, these tablets are chemical and as such lack other elements necessary for proper utilization. Even a B-complex vitamin tablet provides only the chemical *non-food* vitamins. In this case vegetarians are not supplementing their diet with food B-12, but are supplying their diet with B-12 from a *non-food* source because they cannot get it from the foods they choose to eat. A diet so lacking in such a vital element is dangerous.

Vegetables are also very low in iron which, working with B-12, supplies the pizazz in your blood stream. Look closely at many vegetarians and you find many tired people. Liver and other organ meats are the richest sources of iron. Blackstrap molasses, parsley, spinach, and a few others supply some iron, but not usually enough to meet all your blood needs. Certainly a healthy diet should not produce anemia. A proper diet should supply totally what the body needs and should not have to rely on chemical sources for nutritional elements that are missing in the food selection.

Not so long ago another problem for the vegetarian was revealed in a popular health magazine. A report was quoted as saying that cereals contain a high amount of phytic acid, which chelates or leaches certain minerals from the body. Calcium and zinc are two of these minerals. Phytic acid prevents calcium, what little there is in vegetables, from being used by the body. A trace mineral, zinc has been identified as taking part in more bodily functions than any other substance next to calcium. This mineral loss is a condition worth noting, especially since vegetarians eat so much cereal and cereal products.

Vegetarianism has become a very strong and popular food movement. Many young people, as well as adults, have adopted this dietary preference. Because of this the vegetarian meat-substitute industry was born. Most health food stores and many supermarkets now have a section for meat substitutes, products which may look like meat products and taste like meat products but contain no animal substance. Unfortunately, a number of these contain monosodium glutamate or some form of refined sugar, artificial flavorings and colorings, and chemical preservatives because these meat substitutes made from soy and textured proteins, taste so bad.

Vegetarians teach us many things that we will incorporate into our new eating regimen. But avoiding animal sources of food is not one of them. Many vegetarians, in fact, do realize the inadequacies of their diet program and include milk and eggs, the two best sources of protein, in their diet. We cannot do less than include raw fruits and vegetables in ours.

Cutting Down

Another popular way to reduce weight involves the cutting-down diet.

"Are you losing weight?"

"Yes."

"How are you doing it?"

"I'm just cutting down on everything."

A person who decides to cut down usually counts the number of calories he consumes. If he takes in fewer calories than normal, he is bound to lose weight. The fewer the calories, the faster his weight loss.

Many diet charts and pamphlets are available to inform the "cut downer" how many calories this or that food contains. In addition, many restaurants offer specially prepared meals for the dieter who is trying to cut down.

Prime target in this process is the goodies—all the sweet treats and in-between snacks that we so often enjoy. Since most goodies are high calorie and carbohydrate sources, we must be aware of their fat-producing potential. It is not necessary, however, to completely cut out all goodies, just eat fewer than normal. Eat one piece of pie instead of two, accept only half the amount of potatoes, cut down on bread, ease back on the cookies and rolls, and don't drink that third or fourth martini. Don't completely disallow all treats, but pretend you have less money for awhile. Your pocketbook may breathe a sigh of relief, and you significantly reduce calories and carbohydrates.

Besides cutting down on goodies, you should curtail everything else you eat. Cut normal portions in half. Don't neglect healthy foods, but eat less. The less food you eat, the more your body will burn its own fat for the energy it needs.

Some people I know insist that a number of small meals are preferable to three large meals. This is the same eating regimen that hypoglycemics follow. These dieters say that if you eat three big meals, because the digestive system is overloaded, you may not use all the food and thus will store part of it as fat. Eating several small meals will tax digestion much less and will minimize the storage of fat.

People who use the cutting-down method commonly face a psychological as well as a physical test: they must deprive themselves of many tasty items and suffer for a time in order to lose weight. The process becomes a form of punishment, a dietary penance for lack of self-discipline. Pangs of hunger must atone for sins of gluttony. In this respect, the diet is as much mental as physical. However, testing of one's will power is usually very satisfying mentally when the individual has successfully reduced to the desired weight.

Apart from the obvious advantages in eliminating excessive food intake, some glaring weaknesses become evident in the cutting-down diet.

In the first place, as we noted earlier in the calorie counting diet, the distinction concerns quantity of calories, not quality. If your cutting-down diet includes substituting *non-foods* for foods, be careful. Substituting a diet drink for a glass of fruit or vegetable juice makes good calorie sense but very poor food sense. Counting calories is permanently helpful only in light of the quality of the calories you are counting.

All foods contain calories, some more than others. The difference lies in whether they are food calories or imitation *non-food* calories. A glass of apple juice may have 50 calories per 8 ounces, but you will be able to use these food calories nourishing your body, and for energy and digestion of other foods. On the other hand, a popular diet drink may include only one calorie per 8 or 12 ounces, but that amount is all non-food and will not perform one useful function in your body. The chemicals in the drink only serve to quench your appetite or thirst with substitute *non-food*. This drink will decisively hinder the assimilation of other foods as well as use your body as a living test tube for the scientific imaginations of the food technologists and advertising specialists.

When dieters cut down on their goodie consumption, they often make no distinction between food and non-food goodies. High calorie *non-food* goodies, white flour and refined sugar treats are profitable only to the large industries that manufacture them. At no time, whether

95

trying to lose weight or maintain weight, should you consume the commercial cakes, candies, pies, and thousands of other sweet sins the American public holds in its fat fingertips. However, the high calorie *food* products, goodies made with whole grain flours and honey, are essential, in small quantities, to your health. It is to your advantage to cut down on these, but don't cut them out entirely. You will suffer for it. People who have done this know what I mean. On the other hand, if you outlaw now and forever all the *non-food* goodies, you will not only reduce your weight problem but also improve your health.

Fats are a popular subject among the overweight. Almost without exception when someone goes on a weight-reducing diet he eliminates fats and oils from his diet. This is a bad mistake. The *raw oils* in the diet are the very foods which feed the oil glands under the skin, which in turn feeds the skin. The dryness or moisture of the skin is greatly dependent on how much oil appears in your diet. Many women who suffer from dry or cracking skin could avoid this condition if they would take their oil internally instead of applying those expensive creams and lotions externally.

Fats are oils which become solid at room temperature. They come in two varieties, saturated and unsaturated. You are probably most familiar with saturated fats. For instance, cholesterol is a saturated fat, the great offender of the arterial system. Heart problems, hardening of the arteries and high blood pressure are just a few of the maladies linked to this saturated fat. But as bad as it is, cholesterol exists in every cell of the body. Cholesterol is a prime constituent of the hormonal system and is most necessary for the production of vitamin D in the body. The ultraviolet rays of the sun stimulate a chemical reaction with the cholesterol stored in the fat glands under the skin, resulting in the production of vitamin D so necessary for calcium assimilation.

Research scientists now tell us that only one-fourth of the total cholesterol in the body comes from the food we eat. The other three-fourths is manufactured by the body itself. But there seems to be a delicate balance between how much cholesterol we consume and how much the body will produce. Apparently the less cholesterol we consume, the more the body produces. The results are in no way conclusive at this time, but they tend to run contrary to many diets and medical opinions. It is most heartening to note that research scientists have identified certain products that will definitely raise the amount of cholesterol stored in the arteries. Coffee, refined sugar, alcohol, white flour, drugs, and cigarettes are just a few. Better to eliminate these *nonfoods* than sacrifice foods that may contain some cholesterol along with healthy partners.

The unsaturated fats are very important for proper brain and nerve functions, and they insure an active, healthy sex life. Lecithin is an unsaturated fat which makes up over 18 percent of the brain, 30 percent of the nervous system, and over 90 percent of the male sperm —certainly not a food you want to eliminate from your diet.

Proper food selection and awareness of food properties are essential for the dieter who merely wants to lessen his food consumption. Ignorance of basic knowledge in this area may lead to unbalanced or even dangerously harmful eating patterns.

Even if it were nutritionally sound, which it is not, eating many small meals instead of three regular meals is not something you can continue for any length of time. Stopping every two hours or so to enjoy a small meal simply does not fit into our life-styles today. Be-

97

sides, if you nibble all day, you stand a very good chance of putting an added strain on your digestive system, which must continuously draw extra blood and nutrients to the digestive organs to break down and assimilate the constant flow of food. Most nibblers I know censure this method because they tend to gain weight rather than lose it.

Most weight loss programs attract participants who are zealous at the beginning of their new program. The *cutting down* dieters, however, very soon wane in their enthusiastic support of the weight loss diet. This is common to most diets, of course, primarily because being overweight is a very emotionally draining experience. The individual must admit deep inside himself that he doesn't look nice being fat. And he can't really cover up the problem with clothes or makeup. I know some who find covenient labels for their problem, but that is a psychological cop-out they use to build up a false self-worth. Actually, they feel very inadequate because they cannot control their own bodies. The zeal with which they attack a new diet is basically prompted by a need to be free from ugly fat.

Such zeal may be an important element for success in weight loss, but it can also make you prey to gimmicks, shots, pills and other fakery. Keep your enthusiasm and desperation high, and let me show you how easy and inexpensive it is to lose weight and lose it permanently.

Notes

1. Morris Fishbein, ed., *The New Illustrated Medical and Health Encyclopedia* (New York: H.S. Stuttman Company, Inc., 1962).
2. Ibid.

chapter nine

So What's New?

Unfortunately, it has been necessary to dwell initially on the negative aspects and shortcomings of the popular diets. Of all the problems they create, the most severe is that you cannot stay on them for any length of time, much less the rest of your life. Did I say the rest of your life? Yes, the rest of your life.

Everybody right now, without exception, regardless of his weight distribution, is following some kind of diet. Why? Because diet, with a capital D, is nothing more than all the things we eat and drink. I didn't say all the *food* we eat and drink, for as we noted earlier, many times we consume *non-food* in place of food. Careful consideration of the problem must center upon elimination of all *non-food* products. Exclude them for the rest of your life, regardless of weight, health or physical disposition. *Non-foods* do not feed the body and thus have no place in your daily meal fare.

The problem with most of us today is that we are seeking some new scientific discovery to provide a miracle way to lose weight without any effort on our part. So what's new? Some of the diets we discussed stem from the approach that basically announces: "Mr. Overweight Person, you have a problem. You are fat. The solution is here, but it is too complicated for you to use by yourself. Therefore, you need professional help." Enter the diet specialists.

However, diet specialists are not needed. You can lose weight and keep it off. The solution to the fat problem is basically very simple. Anyone who honestly wants to lose weight and keep it off permanently can follow this program and realize fantastic results. It has not been perfected in clinical laboratory studies, nor has it been conducted by registered medical specialists. *But it works.*

This program will satisfy your craving for weight reduction and guarantee proper nutrition without expensive frills. However, one ingredient must be present: you must be *desperate*. You have tried other methods; perhaps you lost weight with them but eventually you gained it back. The principle of desperation is your key to opening the door to a new slim you. No gimmicks or pills are necessary—just the *want to*—to lose weight, to take years off your appearance, and to re-enjoy those favorite activities you used to enjoy when you were thinner and younger.

Emily, an 80-year-old grandmother, had been interested in health since her teen years. She read every book on nutrition she could find. Her home library would make many nutritionists and dietitians envious. She exercised at the health spa and played tennis twice a week. In every respect she was informed and bursting with good health. However, she could not lose that extra two inches of loose flesh around her waist. She had tried all the recommended diets in the books and finally decided she would never lose the inches.

When I shared the Right-Way-of-Eating program with her she said it was too simple and would never work. Every day she came into the health spa and every day I urged her to try the Right-Way-of-Eating. After all, I told her, she had nothing to lose except that two inches. I explained that I thought much of her extra weight on her waist was bloat, caused by eating a big meal at night all her life. She insisted it had to be something more complicated or complex.

Finally I won. After three weeks of talking she adopted the Right-Way-of-Eating. In two weeks she was sleeping better and she was really hungry in the morning. Irregularity, a problem she attributed to her age, soon became a thing of the past. In six weeks she lost 10 pounds and one-and-a-half inches off her waist. The only change she made in her life-style was to begin the Right-Way-of-Eating program.

This program has two basic approaches. The first, of course, concerns what you eat. The second approach will be discussed in the next chapter.

Dinner: Eat Light

The most important meal in the Right-Way-of-Eating is *dinner*, the evening meal. Our eating patterns have been conditioned through tradition, social pressures and our high-powered modern style of living. We begin each day by skimping on, or entirely skipping, breakfast.

The Right Way of Eating

Dinner—Light:

   Vegetable salad (many kinds of raw vegetables
      or steamed vegetables for variety)
   Bits of egg, tuna and/or cheese
   Vegetable or fruit juice

Breakfast—Heavy:

Lunch—Medium:

Then we rush through what we call lunch—nibble on snacks and find calmness in bottles or glasses. In the evening we rush home, starved for dinner. We try to make up, in one meal, what we have missed from two. This routine, coupled with the additional "coffee breaks" throughout the day, is nutritional suicide.

In the Right-Way-of-Eating program, dinner is the lightest meal of the day. A light dinner will not only reinforce your change in eating habits but will also improve your physical condition. There are two good reasons why you should eat lightly at night.

The first reason is that eating proteins at night increases the amount of fat you have. Did you hear that? All those great-tasting steak dinners are helping you stay heavy. Remember, over 65 percent of all the proteins you consume is converted into carbohydrates. What carbohydrates you do not use for energy will be stored as fat. At night your activity level is low and your carbohydrate retention is very high. Unnecessary protein will be stored as fat. Because daytime is busytime, you should eat proteins then, not at night. Some proteins take a very long time to properly digest and for their waste products to be properly eliminated.

Heavy night meals discourage restful sleep. This is the second reason why you should eat a light dinner. Next to elimination, inability to sleep seems to be one of our most common problems. When you eat a heavy meal at night your body must work hard to digest the food and eliminate the waste products. Of course, the body does this at all meals but it is much harder at night because the body—externally and internally—is programmed to slow down and rest. That is why we go to sleep. Don't make the body work when it is not necessary. Heavy meals are a habit, not a nutritional necessity. Your body should be fed, not stuffed.

What should you eat at your evening meal? Which foods will give your body maximum benefit?

The most valuable foods you can eat at your evening meal are vegetables. Vegetables, especially if they are organically grown, go a long way toward keeping you fit and making you free from fat.

Eating a raw vegetable salad at night will help complete the digestion of foods you have eaten during the day. Digestion is a complicated and often a long process. Some food that you have eaten earlier in the day may still be in the process of "food becoming flesh." Raw vegetables supply enzymes which aid in the digestion process. Cooking and freezing destroy these enzymes. Only raw foods supply them. Gas and stomach pains are signs that digestion is not as effective as it could be. Raw vegetables can enable you to get more mileage from your food.

Vegetable salads prepare your body for a good night's sleep. Completing the digestion of foods, vegetables will give your body a rest. The salad will allow the great bulk of your daily food to be digested before you go to bed. In this way, the internal organs will truly get the rest they need to get.

Vegetables clean out the system. As vegetables help digest food they also cleanse the intestinal tract. Your intestinal tract serves a double purpose: as an organ of assimilation and as an avenue for elimination. Hard-to-digest foods, like proteins, have many poisons which must be eliminated as digestion waste. At night it is very hard to eliminate these poisons. (Remember, the skin is the number one organ for elimination.) So they are stored, unless you are very active in the middle of the night, in the intestinal tract. Waste stored in the intestines can produce *protein poisoning*, a condition caused by jamming proteins in your body at night over a long period of time. When toxins are not eliminated efficiently, the poison level in the body rises.[1] These toxins are the normal by-product of food digestion—for example carbon dioxide and water—which are left over when food is digested. These toxins are usually eliminated by the kidneys, bowels and skin.

A high retention of waste products, I think, is one of the best ways to age prematurely, because you overtax your body by making it work so hard when it should relax. A more complete digestion of proteins is accomplished during the day when your energy level is high and you are actively engaged in your usual activities.

Cellulose, the indigestible protein in raw vegetables, is the *Drano* for the intestinal tract. It has a churning, cleansing action on the undigested or partly digested food which is lying in the intestinal tract. The blood stream passes right over the intestinal tract absorbing digested food and transporting it to the areas of the body that need it. Undigested food, however, just lies in the intestinal tract and putrefies. This decaying, useless matter interferes with assimilation and creates a garbage-like environment which can support many unhealthy organisms. Cellulose forces waste products down intestines to be eliminated. If you experience some gas when you start on the Right-Way-of-Eating, don't be alarmed and don't give up. This is just the cellulose removing years and years of piled-up wastes. It will take time, but your body is lowering its poison level.

Vegetable salads will help eliminate lower abdominal bloat. A thick midsection—the first place one adds weight and the last place he loses it—is usually the prime catalyst for dieting. This "lower abdominal bloat" is caused by food rotting in the stomach and by faulty elimination. Both are uncomfortable and unhealthy results of eating that big meal at night. If you continue making your stomach and digestive tract a holding-tank for undigested food and their poisons, an overweight condition may be a minor problem confronting you.

The roughage in raw vegetables will help speed up elimination of *non-foods* from your body and strip the insides of the intestinal tract. Through regular consumption, vegetables will assure the least amount of waste deposited in this important organ.

A salad at night will fill you up, not out. Vegetables are very low in weight-gaining calories and fat-forming carbohydrates. You can eat vast amounts of vegetables. Never make a small dinner salad. Make it big with at least eight to ten different kinds of vegetables. Use steamed vegetables and raw vegetables. Most vegetables you would normally cook can be eaten raw. Eating a variety of vegetables (eight or more) will keep this meal from being boring. And just so one vegetable won't dominate the taste, chop them up small and use a good-tasting salad dressing. (Check those labels, however, and be on the alert for any of our *non-food* friends.)

Eat until you are full. If you get hungry after dinner, snack on more vegetables. In doing this, we borrow from the vegetarian's handbook: clean out with vegetables. Instead of taking days or weeks to rid the body of these poisons, we can keep ahead of the game by cleaning out every day.

The Right-Way-of-Eating

Dinner—Light:
   Vegetable salad (many kinds of raw vegetables
      or steamed vegetables for variety)
   Bits of egg, tuna and/or cheese
   Vegetable or fruit juice

Breakfast—Heavy:
   Beef (hamburger, steak, liver, hash, chili,
      spaghetti, roast)
   Egg (Fried, scrambled, omelet, poached, hard-boiled,
      over-easy)
   Whole grain bread or toast or fruit or cereal
   Fruit juice or milk

Lunch—Medium:

Breakfast: Your Most Important Meal

Many of us wake up in the morning with absolutely no desire for food. In fact, the thought of food may even nauseate us. This is because our stomachs are still full from the heavy meal we ate the night before. The steak, potatoes and gravy, and rich dessert are still in our bodies largely unused. Our digestive systems did not get their necessary rest while we slept.

For many years I could not even think about breakfast without feeling sick at my stomach. I ate my biggest meal at night and was still full the next morning. However, when I began eating salads at night, I found I was very hungry in the morning. My body had rested and was now ready for more food. This may not happen to you the first morning after your dinner salad, nothing is harder to lose than an old habit, but soon the food hangover will be replaced by a healthy hunger.

When their parents started eating a big breakfast, Steve and Joan grimaced and plunged back into their sugar-filled, vitamin-fortified commercial cereal. They didn't have time for a big breakfast. Being teenagers, they were always on the go, always hungry, and would eat anything that wasn't moving—except vegetables. Only a salad at night?! After all, they were still growing. They needed a big dinner. Celery, carrots and the like were for animals, not humans. They might eat one or two vegetables on occasion, but not every night and definitely not exclusive of everything else for dinner.

Unlike other diets they had tried, Steve's and Joan's parents were sticking with this one and enjoying it. Mom was losing weight and dad wasn't collapsing on the sofa after dinner. Besides there were fewer dishes to do and longer evenings to enjoy. At night mom just reheated for the kids the meat, spaghetti or whatever, that she and dad had for breakfast.

Steve and Joan decided to try this new way of eating. Within a week Steve and Joan were suggesting new vegetables the family could try in their salad. They began to look forward to dinner for breakfast. They no longer craved the junk in their diets—cokes, candy, pastries—and were rapidly winning their friends at school to this new way of eating. Their parents hadn't pressured them to change their own eating habits, they had just allowed the teenagers to watch the results.

Breakfast literally means "breaking the fast." You have not eaten for 10 to 14 hours; your body has been operating at a reduced rate and your blood sugar level is very low. All this affects your energy level. To raise this energy-supplying blood sugar level, most of us drink a cup of coffee or take nothing at all. You already have been made aware of the many harmful effects of the caffeine in coffee. It raises the blood sugar level, but, since it is a *non-food*, it cannot maintain a healthy energy level and thus provokes a drowsy droop. We need food to wake up our bodies and turn droop to drive.

Besides the daily energy supply you need, you must also furnish your body with the raw material necessary to rebuild and repair body tissues you use in normal activity.

We are all creatures of habits formed from childhood by the intentional and unintentional influences of our parents. But habits can be changed. If we inaugurate a profitable habit of eating a heavy breakfast, we will establish eating habits for the other meals. Each meal reinforces the next meal. Most people get the 10 o'clock droopies because there is insufficient fuel in their bodies. They may draw on protein reserves, but these reserves are not inexhaustible.

It has been proved countless times that employees function much better with a good breakfast in their bellies. The brain uses a tremendous amount of food fulfilling all of its obligations to keep us breathing, digesting, moving and thinking. Thus it is critical that we continue supplying the master computer with the best food possible.

The best food possible in the morning is some form of protein. Protein maintains blood sugar at a higher level for a longer period of time. The great American breakfast attempts to supply this needed source of protein by offering bacon or some other pork product. Pork is not the best source of protein for our breakfast needs for two reasons, at least.

First, pork is extremely fatty—too fatty for the person who wants to lose weight.

Second, pigs are indiscriminate eaters and their diets consist of almost everything they can get their snouts into. Whatever they eat is digested and added to their bodies as flesh in a very short period of time, without much straining or filtering out of body poisons. So, for the most part, these poisons are deposited on the body of the animal and passed on to you when you eat pork. It is not unusual for people to get very ill after eating a pork product. I personally think pork products are really *non-foods* because of their debilitating effects on your system.

Beef is one of the best foods for a morning meal. And because it is one of the hardest proteins to digest, you should eat it in the morning so your body has all day to digest it and properly eliminate the poisonous by-products of digestion.

Since beef is hard to digest, it will not instantly skyrocket the blood sugar level like coffee and donuts will. But this is what you want. For the quicker the blood sugar level raises, the quicker it drops. The tough tissue in the beef is broken down slowly and maintains a good energy level. It stays with you longer, literally, so that your body can continually draw on this food for energy, building material and emergency supply.

A beef patty, liver, or steak will also help depress your appetite until noon. The 10 o'clock coffee break, you see, is conveniently timed to try to counteract the droop from the businessman's anemic breakfast. Beef depresses your appetite by adequately nourishing your body. Thus you will not run on nervous energy. What is nervous energy? There are two kinds of energy—food energy and nervous energy. You already know what food energy is. Nervous energy, on the other hand, is a negative kind of energy that is gained now at the expense of your body later. Sometimes, in times of emergency or stress, nervous energy is very helpful. When you really need it your mind forces your body to stay awake or perform when it really shouldn't or can't. However, you should not rely upon nervous energy to replace the food you should be eating. People with a lot of aggressive drive, who push themselves beyond what is healthy, are often victims of nervous energy. The "nervous energy" type individuals are people who often have serious heart attacks or sudden illness without prior history of heart trouble. They drain themselves, without eating proper food and getting sufficient rest, until their bodies can't function any longer under the stress.

When you are literally starving at mid-morning, you can get jittery or hypernervous, depending on your particular temperament. If you start your day with beef your appetite will be depressed until noon, keeping the blood sugar level even.

Now that the beef is broiling, let's cook up an egg or two. The protein of the egg is the very best protein you can eat. Scientists grade proteins by biological value— how well the body can utilize each protein. The biological value of egg protein, the albumin found in the white part of the egg, can be assimilated more fully than any other protein you can eat—over 97 percent in a healthy body. Milk, beef and fish follow eggs.

Many people don't include eggs in their diet because of the high amounts of cholesterol found in them. Cholesterol, the heart and artery offender, seems to be the scare of the seventies; however, remember those salient scientific facts we discussed earlier? Three-fourths of all the cholesterol in your body is manufactured *by your body*. Only one-fourth comes from the food. So by completely cutting out all cholesterol-containing foods, only one-fourth of the total will be affected. Don't cut out eggs until you have removed all other *non-foods* that can raise cholesterol levels.

Until 60 years ago only one kind of egg was available commercially. Now we hear of regular eggs and fertile eggs. Which should we eat? Is there really a difference? Years ago, when we as a country were not yet blessed with sophisticated mechanization and high-speed living, chickens were allowed to run free on the ground, scratch the soil for minerals, eat a nutritious non-chemical diet, lead a normal sex life with roosters, and not be part of an assembly line production. Force feeding, artificial lighting, growth hormones, no soil scratching, and an absence of roosters is now the fate for chickens on most of today's egg ranches. This type of environment seriously affects the quality of the eggs we buy. If the chickens don't scratch, the eggs they produce may well be lacking in many important minerals. Growth hormones and *non-food* will not produce nutritious eggs.

The worst part of the hen's lot, however, is the absence of the roosters. In times past they were always there. From the rooster's sperm the hen gets lecithin, the life-giving substance so necessary for reproduction.

This *lecithin*, incidentally, *is also the natural counter-balance for cholesterol.* As long as the hen has been fertilized by the rooster—hence the name fertile eggs—the lecithin will be present to emulsify the cholesterol so that your body can use it and keep the cholesterol from settling in the arteries.

One more comment about eggs. Let's draw a comparison that may seem a little crude but will further illustrate why you should eat fertile eggs. Hens will lay eggs whether there are roosters around or not. That is their normal function. In similar fashion, a woman every month lays an egg. If it is not fertilized by the man's sperm, she casts it off as waste during her period. This is also what the hen does. Since the hen was not fertilized by the rooster, the infertile eggs are waste products. She will not sit on these infertile eggs because she knows they will never produce life. Waste products are not high quality food.

We now have two sources of protein for breakfast. We should also include some form of carbohydrates since they help to assimilate protein better. Carbohydrates are energy, nothing more, and energy is what we need in the morning. The body will have no trouble burning up these carbohydrates during the day.

To give yourself variety, eat whole grain bread some mornings and fresh fruit other mornings. One or the other will definitely help to satisfy your sweet craving. Protein and fats will supply carbohydrates indirectly but your body still needs some nutritious food carbohydrates. Whole grain bread supplies minerals and other food factors which are not found in other foods. Since it is not refined down to commercial white flour, you are getting the whole food. Make sure when choosing your whole grain bread that you read the label closely. It should not contain white flour, enriched white flour, refined sugar, syrups, preservatives, additives or other *non-food* products. Do not be fooled by the name of a bread or a so-called name brand. Look at the label and discover what is inside the loaf.

Fresh fruit in season is hard to beat. Fruits are concentrated sources of energy. Almost totally carbohydrates, they will raise the blood sugar quickly and the protein will keep it there. Besides the carbohydrates, fresh raw fruit is loaded with enzymes, which help to digest all the food you are eating. If our bodies were automobiles on a used car lot, most of us would sit there until the paint fell off our fenders. No one would buy us because of our poor gas mileage. We are very inefficient, often because much of what we eat is just stacked in the intestinal tract.

Coffee is out—fruit juice is in. Fresh fruit juice will not dilute the digestive juices in the stomach or wash away the unstable nutrients in our food as coffee will.

Raw juice is much better than heated juice. Remember, any juice that you find on the shelves unrefrigerated must have been heated sometime or it would go bad very quickly. The heating process destroys the enzymes and makes the juice last longer. You should also be aware that many juices and *all drinks* include some kind of *non-food* additive like syrup or refined sugar. Stay away from these. Raw juice is healthiest, supplying the same basic nutrients found in the raw fruits and vegetables.

For variety have milk for breakfast. Milk affords some carbohydrates but it is also the second best source of protein. And since you are eliminating all the *non-food* from your diet, drink certified raw milk rather than pasteurized milk. Pasteurized milk is not really milk at all. It is a by-product of milk, the residue left after milk has been cooked.

Our fathers, grandfathers, and great grandfathers grew up on milk "right from the cow." How did they do without pasteurized milk? Pasteurization was first employed in France because farmers had a serious problem with cleanliness in their dairy industry. So instead of cleaning up the dairy industry, they kept the conditions the same and sterilized the milk. The pasteurization process kills all the harmful bacteria for a time but it also destroys the acid-forming, good bacteria which helps keep in check the disease-carrying bacteria. This burnt-out liquid becomes a fertile breeding ground for bacteria. Here are some facts to help you determine what milk is best for you:

1. The bacteria count in certified raw milk is much lower than in pasteurized milk.

2. Certified raw milk contains no pathogenic bacteria. Pasteurized milk is *usually safe* from pathogens. (That's reassuring isn't it?)

3. Certified raw milk will eventually sour and can then be used to make other dairy products. Pasteurized milk will not sour. It goes rancid, and rancid is not palatable.

4. Because certified raw milk has not been cooked it contains all the enzymes. One of these enzymes is phosphatase. This is the enzyme necessary for the proper assimilation of phosphorous which works hand in hand with calcium. In pasteurized milk only 10 percent of the enzymes are available.

5. You can assimilate the protein in certified raw milk so much better because heat has not altered the amino acid structure of the protein. Several of the essential amino acids have been partially destroyed.

6. All 18 fatty acids are in certified raw milk. Cholesterol can be digested because lecithin has not been cooked out as it has been in pasteurized milk.

7. All the vitamins are available in certified raw milk to nourish the body. They are not left in the bottom of the pasteurization vat.

If you cannot find certified raw milk in your area, perhaps you can get it shipped in. If not, drink fresh juices, find a sympathetic farmer, or make your own from non-instantized milk powder. Certified raw milk is the best you can drink, but do the best you can.

The-Right-Way-of-Eating

Dinner—Light:
   Vegetable salad (many kinds of raw vegetables
      or steamed vegetables for variety)
   Bits of egg, tuna and/or cheese
   Vegetable or fruit juice

Breakfast—Heavy:
   Beef (hamburger, steak, liver, hash, chili,
      spaghetti, roast)
   Egg (fried, scrambled, omelet, poached, hard-boiled,
      over easy)
   Whole grain bread or toast or fruit or cereal
   Fruit juice or milk

Lunch—Medium:
   Fish or fowl (piece of chicken or turkey; tuna,
      chicken or turkey sandwich—if you had no bread
      for breakfast; tuna, chicken or turkey salad or
      casserole)
   Cottage cheese, yogurt or cheese
   Raw vegetable or fruit
   Milk or juice

Lunch: More High-Quality Protein

A heavy breakfast will become a habit that will definitely alter your eating habits. The heavy, hard-to-digest protein will eliminate the need to snack and will keep the blood sugar at a high energy level. Now instead of skipping or skimping on lunch, we need to eat more high quality protein to maintain our energy throughout the afternoon and keep supplying the body with raw material to rebuild the tissue we are wearing down through normal work and play.

Fish or fowl satisfy this protein requirement. Fish and fowl are high quality sources of protein and, unlike beef, they are much easier to digest. The minimum daily requirement for protein is not very high, but it is considerably higher than what most people get in their normal diets. A minimum daily requirement is the amount of a nutrient a person needs each day to prevent deficiency. This computed amount is by no means an optimum level. And yet when it comes to protein, many barely reach these minimum levels.

Eating a heavy protein breakfast and a medium protein lunch will give you well over the minimum amount of protein and you will observe the results of this protein consumption in the improved condition of your nails, hair, eyes, complexion, skin and energy level. I keep hammering away at your energy level for one reason: if your diet does not supply you with enough energy to carry on your normal functions and anything extra, it invites snacking and diet cheating. By contrast we provide a new set of eating habits that fits any life-style and discourages snacking and cheating because you are feeding your body properly.

That big breakfast will definitely curtail your hunger at lunch. But eat lunch, otherwise the salad at dinner will not satisfy you. The easily digestible protein eaten at lunch will be sufficiently digested by the time you go to bed.

Along with the fish or fowl, eat cottage cheese, cheese, or yogurt. All these foods contain some protein as well as carbohydrates to help digest the protein and other foods. Remember again, carbohydrates are fuel. If you are active, you will use up this fuel.

Cottage cheese has long been heralded as the dieter's *must food,* so most dieters grudgingly include it in one of their meals. We must admit that it serves as a good source of protein and is very low in calories, but it is not a wonder food to be eaten at the expense of other good foods. Include it on a fairly regular basis. But you don't have to eat it every day.

Cheese—raw cheese if possible—is also a good source of protein. Most of us enjoy the sweet taste of cheese and there is no reason to eliminate it from your food selection. Cheese is a milk product and thus one of the best proteins available. It is not as rich a source of protein as milk, but it belongs in the same family.

Yogurt is one of those foods that supposedly belongs to the health kooks and faddists. Many claims have been made for it, and considerable misunderstanding surrounds its content and function. Yogurt is a thick, curdled milk product to which bacteria is added. This bacteria, lactobacillus acidophilus or bulgarius, is very beneficial to the intestinal tract, the area where much of the food is finally digested and waste products removed. Your intestines need to maintain a high bacteria level so that they can effectively curtail the growth of harmful, disease-producing bacteria. These injurious bacteria are always present and antibiotics or drugs can multiply them in the warm environ of the digestive tract, or by large amounts of food passing through. If your digestion is not too efficient and you do not properly eliminate

117

waste, real intestinal problems can result.

The bacteria in yogurt is rich fertilizer for the production of good intestinal bacteria. If you eat yogurt or drink kefir (yogurt with juice added to make a drink), you assure yourself a healthy level of intestinal bacteria. I would not eat yogurt every day, however. The bacteria has a stripping effect on the insides of the digestive tract; daily ingestion may clean your system too much and create loose bowels. Eat yogurt on a regular basis but vary it with cottage cheese or cheese.

An absolute requisite for lunch is some sort of raw vegetable. Almost anywhere you eat, you will find some raw vegetables. Again variety is a good plan to follow. Experiment with many vegetables. For different vegetables supply varying amounts of vitamins and minerals. The important thing is that they be raw.

Now to finish off lunch, drink a glass of raw milk or fruit or vegetable juice. Either choice will satisfy your thirst in conjunction with good food. This lunch will certainly carry you quite nicely until dinner and that large vegetable salad.

Once you make salads a regular habit for dinner, you will feel quite sluggish when you skimp on lunch and have a heavy dinner. There will be times when you are invited out to dinner or you miss a meal and are so hungry that the salad will not do. When this happens do not give up the ship. You have not ruined your diet. You have not done the best but you can make an adjustment. You can use the *principle of compensation*. If you eat a heavy dinner, eat less the next day and do more of the X-factor (see next chapter).

No-Time-to-Eat Drink
   8 oz. unsweetened fruit juice
   1 raw egg

    1 scoop honey ice cream
    2 tbsp. unsweetened protein powder
Pour juice in blender. Add 1 egg and 1 scoop of honey ice cream. Turn blender on low and add protein powder. Switch on high speed for five seconds and turn off. If you blend drink too long you will have more foam than drink. This drink will supply between 20-35 grams of protein, depending on the kind of protein powder you use.

Six-Day Salad

Nutritionally, it is best to eat vegetables as soon as they are sliced or peeled. Unfortunately this is not always possible. If you are like me, you simply don't have time to make a salad every night. So, on Saturday or Sunday, I make a large salad to last the whole week. If you use a wide variety of vegetables and chop or grate them into small pieces, you will not be overpowered by one taste. Tomatoes, alfalfa sprouts and mung bean sprouts should not be added to the six-day salad but should be added nightly. Also, if you want bits of cheese, tuna or hard-boiled eggs in your salad, add this nightly.

Following is a list of some of the more common vegetables you can put in your six-day salad:

alfalfa sprouts	leeks
carrots	mushrooms
cauliflower	mung bean sprouts
celery	onions
comfrey	radishes
cucumbers	red bell peppers
escarole	red cabbage
garlic	red lettuce
green bell peppers	spinach
green cabbage	tomatoes
iceberg lettuce	

Foods to Feast On

Flours—all whole grain: wheat, buckwheat, soy, rye; NO white, refined or fortified flours.

Breads—all whole grain without refined flours, refined sugars, preservatives, chemicals or synthetic vitamins.

Cereals—all whole grain cereals that do not contain synthetic vitamins, chemical additives, refined flours or sugars.

Garden goodies—all fruits and vegetables.

Meat—chicken; beef; turkey; fish. NO pork, lobster, crab or scavengers.

Dairy—raw milk; raw cheese; raw butter; non-sugared yogurt; non-sugared kefir; fertile eggs.

Snacks—nuts (all kinds); seeds (pumpkin, sunflower, sesame); honey ice cream; candies, cakes and pastries without sugar or refined flours.

Drinks—non-sugared fruit and vegetable juices; raw milk; herb teas; spring water.

Note

1. John H. Tilden, *Toxemia: The Basic Causes of Disease* (Chicago: Natural Hygiene Press, 1974).

Sample Menu for the Right-Way-of-Eating

(**Bold** type indicates increased portion for men)

Dinner Each Day
salad
vegetable or fruit juice (8 oz.)

Breakfast	Lunch
MONDAY	
beef patty (4 oz.) **(6 oz.)**	baked cod (sm. piece)
1 poached egg	**(med. piece)**
piece of fruit	2 oz. cottage cheese
8 oz. fruit juice	celery sticks
	8 oz. milk
TUESDAY	
stew (sm. portion)	broiled halibut (4 oz.)
(med. portion)	**(6 oz.)**
1 slice whole grain bread	1 cheese slice
8 oz. milk	carrot stick
	8 oz. milk
WEDNESDAY	
steak (4 oz.) **(6 oz.)**	tuna salad (4 oz.) **(6 oz.)**
scrambled eggs (1 or 2) **(2)**	yogurt (4 oz.)
8 oz. fruit juice	radishes
	8 oz. milk
THURSDAY	
liver (4 oz.) **(6 oz.)**	broiled swordfish (4 oz.)
cooked vegetable	**(6 oz.)**
8 oz. milk	2 oz. cottage cheese
	small cucumber
	8 oz. juice
FRIDAY	
spaghetti (sm. portion)	baked chicken breast (1)
(med. portion)	yogurt (4 oz.)
1 slice whole grain bread	carrot sticks
8 oz. fruit juice	8 oz. milk

121

SATURDAY

roast beef (4 oz.)	turkey slices (4 oz.)
(6 oz.)	**(6 oz.)**
½ baked potato	celery sticks
vegetable	cottage cheese (2 oz.)
8 oz. milk	8 oz. milk

SUNDAY

meat (4 oz.) **(6 oz.)**	tuna fish sandwich
cheese omelet (2 eggs)	carrots
8 oz. fruit juice	8 oz. milk

part four

The Missing Element

chapter ten
The X-Factor

chapter eleven
How Do I Begin?

chapter twelve
It Works; Try It

chapter ten
The X-Factor

The first step to feeling *Fit and Free* is to eat the right way. The second step is one you hear and read little about in weight-loss books. This second step is one we don't like to talk about, much less use. Yet the reason most people roam from diet to diet and go from loss to gain throughout their whole lives is because they don't include this X-factor or else they don't utilize it with the same fervor they muster for each new miracle diet. If they did they would realize their goals permanently, as long as they continued to use the X-factor.

What is the X-factor? *Exercise, Exercise, Exercise!* The great equalizer. Eating a heavy breakfast, medium lunch and light dinner will not move muscles, keep busts from falling, rear ends from drooping or shoulders from sagging. Exercise will. Athletes are perfect examples of this principle. Even though many of them have poor eating habits, some drink, smoke and take drugs, the exercise in which they engage allows their bodies to compensate for their abusive habits.

Unfortunately, exercise is not included in modern diet plans because most of us are basically lazy when it comes to this part of the program. In fact, some special diets loudly proclaim that their weight-loss programs do *not* require any strenuous exercise at all. Rather, if you follow their program, the weight just peels off. We are inundated with the idea that exercise is completely useless when it comes to losing weight, thus exercise-haters convince the majority of overweight people that exercise for weight loss is, at best, of secondary importance. The diet is most important.

Sharon had been on the Right-Way-of-Eating plan for six months. She felt so good eating light meals at night that many of her dates received lectures on the harmful effects of eating meat at night. She came to the spa three times a week where I was working but she wouldn't exercise. She used the sauna and steam and did a wee bit of swimming, but no exercise.

Sharon was blessed with a naturally healthy and trim body. Except for some physical education in high school she had done little exercise. She hated exercise. Her interests were mental, not physical. But now, at 38, she couldn't lose 10 pounds she had gained over the summer and her lower back still pained her from an injury she suffered while trying to move her piano. I don't know how many hours I talked to her before she finally agreed to go on an exercise program. Much to her surprise exercise wasn't as bad as she thought. Soon she lost 10 pounds, strengthened her back and really began to develop confidence in herself, her physical self. Her body was more flexible and she began using muscles she never knew she had.

Your body stores fat around muscles that are least used. Your whole body receives the distribution of fat cells, but they are usually heaviest in the middle of the body; waist, abdomen, hips, upper thighs and rear end. We exercise these areas so seldom.

When you lose weight by changing your diet without adding exercise, the fat globules reduce in size, but they remain. In time they may mat down, over, under and through the muscle tissue. This is often what has happened to a woman who has heavy thighs that seem very muscular and hard to the touch but are dimpled and fatty in appearance. Call it any name you like but *it is still fatty tissue that has not been removed.* The longer you carry it, the harder it is to remove. But *you* put it on, so *you* can take it off.

How Does Exercise Help?

Contracting muscles during any kind of muscular exercise causes acids to be secreted by the muscles. These acids in turn burn off the fatty tissue around the muscles you are exercising. Eating will not promote the secretion of these fat-burning acids. Food composes these acids but only exercise forces their use.

As the acids burn off the fatty cells, your muscles get stronger and harder. A lack of exercise causes just the opposite effect. Weak and soft muscles perform inefficiently and make you look much older than you are. Your face muscles sag with extra weight and your lung cage and shoulders droop forward from weak postural muscles. Diet alone will not correct this.

Jean lost 85 pounds by starving herself and taking diet pills. All over her body her skin hung in great globs of "cottage-cheese" flesh. I have seldom seen a more sloppy body. When she walked she shimmied and shook like a bowl of Jello. She had no energy and was starting to gain her weight back.

If she had followed a regular exercise program this condition could have been avoided. She finally did start to exercise but it was an unnecessarily tough battle to rid herself of the matted tissue that covered her from neck to knees.

Because of a desire to do anything as easily as possible, we make losing weight more and more complex. We develop this system or that system; we eat special foods, adhere to strict diets and count everything. But the fact remains, we still must exercise those muscles to burn off fat and develop good muscle tissue.

Exercise eliminates body toxins. Even when you exclude all *non-foods* from your diet you are not free from toxins. It takes time for your body to reflect the effects of abuse and it takes even longer for it to regenerate itself. Toxins remain in the fat tissue. For example, if you recently quit smoking, don't expect to completely eradicate all poisonous residues and disabling effects smoking has had on your body. This process takes time. Be patient and consistent in your exercise.

In addition to the many ways we deliberately abuse our bodies, we are constantly bombarded by poisons from the air we breathe. There is no place on earth to escape air pollution, although some areas have less pollutants than others.

Toxins occur as a natural by-product of cell nourishment. When you digest your food, waste is inevitable, and waste, such as carbon dioxide, must be eliminated.

Exercise helps you eliminate waste from your body through your skin, the number one organ for elimination. When you exercise strenuously you perspire.

127

Many toxins are removed through perspiration. A good exercise program, concentrating on your waist and abdominal areas, will develop strong internal stomach muscles that will produce sufficient secretions for digestion and strong intestinal and colon muscles to move the body waste to the excretion area.

Jack was troubled with poor digestion. Most foods, even non-spicy ones, gave him gas. He munched on antacid tablets and tried different preparations to help his constipation. Jack had a 38-inch waist on a 5-foot 10-inch frame. He was at least 40 pounds overweight and most of it was centered in the middle of his body. The sides of his waist were heavy and he had a "pot belly."

When Jack came to us we designed a waist program to reduce his waist. In three months his weight dropped 35 pounds and his waist measurement decreased by five inches. He now has a slim, muscular midsection. For the first time in his life he can see stomach muscles. And his digestion? He has stopped using antacid tablets and he has no problem with irregularity.

Exercise increases and improves circulation. For instance, leg exercises will increase the blood supply to that part of the body. The heart responds by pumping harder because a more than normal supply of blood is needed to remove the wastes of muscle activity and fill the demands for nourishment to the muscle cells which are being used. The arteries and capillaries dilate or increase in size to accommodate the extra load of blood. You may experience a "flushing" feeling as the circulation is speeded up. The increase assures quick removal of waste and helps clear veins, arteries and capillaries that may have accumulated unwanted deposits of calcium or fat globules. A widened blood stream is like an efficient freeway system. Things go from here to there in the shortest possible time with the least amount of trouble.

Pam had cold feet. No matter what the temperature her feet never got warm. She also had aches in her calves and ankles. Lower leg exercises greatly improved her circulation and erased ankle and calf pain. She can now sleep with her feet outside the covers.

Exercise will even improve precarious mental health. It is much better to work off frustrations, anxieties and tensions in a good exercise program than to take tranquilizers, alcohol or aspirin. And at the same time you are peeling off extra weight.

Gary was one of those nervous people you sometimes meet. Every little pressure seemed to send him up the wall. He was an accountant and tax season made his ulcer flare up. He lived on pills to calm down, pills to keep him going and medicine for his stomach.

A radical change in eating habits—including, in his diet, foods he previously avoided—and a regular, progressive exercise program produced a dramatic change in Gary's life. His ulcer disappeared along with his pills and medicine. In their place was a calmer, happier and much less nervous accountant.

"If you don't use it, you lose it." Nothing could be more true about your body. In the twenties and sometimes early thirties, your body is young and alive, not primarily because you are young, but because you are using your body. You play hard and are physically active. But this changes as you grow older. Although your body never gets a vacation, seldom rests and runs 24 hours a day, you expect it to perform at top condition all the time. And what do *you* do to get these results? Usually very little.

I think it is safe to say that we are in the middle of an anti-exercise craze. We want to lose weight or stay in good shape, but *please, no exercise.* I can hear you say, "Isn't hard work exercise?"

Many overweight people develop the notion that if they work hard, they will get enough exercise. However, most housewives work hard every day but many also have a difficult time keeping their weight where they would like it. Their arduous tasks simply do not exercise those areas which need it the most. A regular exercise program is an absolute prerequisite for firm muscles.

Those who work the 9-5 standard American job find numerous opportunities for mental exercise but little opportunity for physical exertion. The mind grows better with use and so does the body. Fat midsections and low energy levels are inevitable consequence of our high-mental/low-physical way of life.

What Is Exercise?

Exercise can be described as any activity that one does specifically and primarily for the body. Exercise is a muscle movement designed to improve health, increase endurance, develop strength, enlarge muscles, lose weight, gain weight, or in some way improve the appearance or condition of your body.

Exercise is an end in itself, not a means to an end. Let me clarify. When you lift a heavy box at work, you use your back, shoulders, arms and leg muscles to perform the activity. Your muscles receive some exercise because you have to lift the box; not because you wish to exercise your back, shoulders, arms and leg muscles. If you didn't have to lift the box, you would have omitted the work. You use certain muscles in swinging a pick. You use these muscles in order to break up the dirt. But you lift the pick to perform work and not to exercise muscles. Even though you do realize muscle exercise, that was not your primary intention.

Without further belaboring the point, we must emphasize the fact that although hard, physical work is good for overall health (both mental and physical), it is not usually an activity we would use primarily and effectively for losing weight.

You can get exercise in many ways, most of them quite inexpensive. Jogging, swimming, calisthenics, gymnastics, weight lifting, and bike riding are just a few. But what kind of exercise is best for losing weight and improving physical condition?

Good exercise is goal-oriented. Since you are reading this book, you have expressed a desire to lose weight. That is your goal—to lose weight. But you should be a little more specific. Look at yourself closely in the mirror and decide what parts of your body are most in need of attention. Do your thighs and hips bulge in your capris? Does your sports coat fail to hide the desk droop of your midsection? Whatever your fat problem, view it critically, realizing that you put it there but that proper diet and exercise will remove it.

After labeling your problem areas, measure your: waist____; hips____; thighs____. This is not a complete taping of your body, for we are only concerned with areas that provide problems for most people. Once we return hips, thighs, buttocks and waist areas to acceptable sizes, we can then attack other problems.

In setting your goal, decide how much you want to lose. In establishing that objective, be more concerned with the measurement of a body part than with your total body weight. Weight charts can be misleading. In fact, we can safely assume that if you think you should shed 10 pounds, you probably should lose closer to 20 pounds.

A rather accurate indicator of potential weight loss is the size of your waist. Male or female, young or old, the

131

first place you gain and the last place you lose is your waist area.

Since I cannot see you, I cannot advise you properly concerning waistline. Once in your life, however, you should reduce in weight to the point where you can look in the mirror and see muscles in your abdominal area. This is your base muscular weight. You may never completely remove all the fat from your waist, but you should try to get those "love handles" down and flatten the stomach. A goal of this nature will keep your interest and drive going much longer than reaching your "ideal weight" represented by one of the many standard weight charts.

To be truly effective, exercise must be regular. An occasional jog around the block or a weekend tennis date may make you the pride of the office or the envy of your overweight friends, but it will not offer the results you desire. Fat is a little like cement. When you first make up cement, it is liquid and easily moved. But after it has set for a while, nothing short of chisel and hammer can break or remove it from its resting place. Likewise, if you gain five pounds after an enjoyable summer vacation or short holiday, you can usually lose this extra weight in a very short time. The fat has not yet set on your body, nor has the body been programmed to feed this extra tissue. But the longer the situation continues, the harder it is to shed the unwanted weight. As I have already mentioned more than once, the best time to lose weight is as soon as you have gained it. For this reason, regular exercise is the chisel that will break down fatty tissue and eliminate excess baggage.

Exercise will also alter your eating requirements. At first regular exercise may stimulate your appetite because of the new energy output. But as fat is broken down by muscle activity, you will not have as much body to feed. You would be amazed how much food is needed to feed an extra 10 pounds.

Exercise can be harmful and downright dangerous if it is not pursued on a regular basis. The weekend golfer or once-a-month baseball star can attest to the soreness and disability he endures on Monday morning, primarily because his exercise level is close to nothing during the week. I recently read a story about a middle-aged doctor who dropped dead while jogging with a doctor friend. Shortly after that, a deluge of articles presented the dangerous side of exercise. Exercise itself is not dangerous. We make exercise hazardous by expecting and demanding too much from our underused bodies.

Only when exercise is performed on a regular basis will you firm muscles and increase the endurance and stamina of your body. Any exercise can be used to increase endurance and cardiovascular efficiency. Contrary to what some authorities believe, running and jogging are not the only means available to make the heart and lungs stay young. Weight loss and improved circulation can go hand in hand, but only when exercise is performed on a regular basis.

Exercise must be hard. The degree of intensity depends on how long you have been doing a particular kind of exercise. Obviously a man who has been jogging for six months can exercise much harder than a man who has just started to jog. But it is all relative. In the beginning you are weak and out of condition. You cannot do very much. As time goes on, you get stronger, and so your exercise can become harder too.

At all times your exercise program must be hard. Muscles that are not forced to exercise as hard as possible will not gain the tightness and firmness you desire. *As hard as possible* is the essential guideline for every exercise. If I just play or take it easy during my workout,

I have not done my body justice. At times, of course, you cannot work out as hard as you would like, but proceed as hard as you can under the circumstances.

It is very important that you concentrate on what you're doing. If your mind is not focused on the exercise being performed, you are merely going through the motions. Success in exercise is like success in any endeavor: train all your attention on the task at hand; think what the muscle is doing, even imagine how it moves. Do not have anything else on your mind. For the half hour or hour you exercise, block out all the rest of the world. It never ceases to amaze me how I can do the same exercise, in the same style, with the same resistance, but feel it so much more when I really concentrate on the movement. When you concentrate on your exercise, you allow your brain to unlock power you would not otherwise have while daydreaming or remaining preoccupied with outside activities. Only then can you exercise as hard as possible.

Exercise must be done correctly. Many people do not receive the results they expect from their exercise. This is not the fault of the exercise, for to get full benefits from any exercise movement, you must do it correctly. Find out exactly how the exercise is supposed to be done and then do not veer from that style. It may do your ego good to cheat and add more resistance, but the muscles are not so easily fooled. Your time is so precious that it is foolish to waste it. By doing the exercise correctly, you will get more benefits in a shorter period of time.

Peggy had been exercising for years. But it had done little to improve her appearance. She was 5-feet 4-inches tall and weighed 140 pounds. Even though she exercised regularly she couldn't lose weight and get "those inches off." She adopted the Right-Way-of-Eating program and a new way of exercising.

Her problem had been two-fold: first, her exercise was too general; second, she had a problem concentrating. We began an exercise program that concentrated her energy on particular problem areas. We focused on her hips and thighs, then, as we saw the inches come off, we centered our attention on her waist. In just 10 weeks she showed more results than she had the previous 10 years.

Exercise must also be progressive. Next to making your exercise program a regular habit, this is the most important quality of good exercise or weight loss. The exercise program should be such that the intensity of the workouts increases as time goes on. Instead of running for 10 minutes, run 15 minutes; instead of 100 twists, do 200 twists, rather than 100 pounds for eight repetitions, do 110 pounds for eight repetitions.

The body becomes accustomed to the amount of resistance in the form of whatever exercise you are doing and must have added resistance to receive further healthful benefits. This progressive resistance is usually associated with weight lifting, but it can be adapted to any kind of exercise. Here are some examples.

1. Jogging. You have been jogging three days a week for a distance of three miles each day. Your next jogging day, you run the last 100 yards as fast as you can. The following week you sprint 110 yards. Then continue this progression until you are running the whole three miles at a fast clip. You can then change from distance running to time running. That is, run 20 minutes and increase it so many times per week.

2. Calisthenics or freehand exercise. If you are doing freehand exercises, you can increase the number of repetitions or the speed at which you do them, or you can decrease the amount of rest between sets of exercise. Again the emphasis is on progressive resistance.

3. Exercise with weights. Weightlifting movements

can be increased most easily by adding more weight. The strength of whatever muscles you are using increases as the weight mounts so long as you do the movement correctly. As your muscles get stronger, you can accomplish more work.

Strong muscles are trim, hard muscles. You will find that most people who are grossly overweight do not have strength commensurate with their body poundage. As you exercise progressively, muscles gain strength and burn off fatty tissue. The only way to permanently lose fat is by contracting your muscles.

I have heard many people say, "Well I'm just doing enough to stay in shape. I don't want to become a fanatic." This is not true. You don't stay in shape. You either get better or get worse. You may not put on weight, but your flesh may be a little more flabby, your endurance considerably less, or your body more tired. This is not staying in shape. A little fanaticism will keep you from becoming a national statistic.

Exercise designed to help you lose weight will also enable you to get in better shape. But as your body becomes accustomed to a certain level of energy output, it stops improving. Exercise must be progressive to insure continuing results. A mile runner runs longer distances to make sure his legs and lungs can be called upon for a last lap sprint. Your waistline stays small and muscular only as you work it harder each time. If you do 10 sit-ups and never increase the resistance, your stomach muscles will never shed themselves of that extra fatty tissue. Progressive resistance, remember can be accomplished by adding more repetitions, more sets, more weight resistance, or shorter rest periods. However you do it, progressive exercise will enable you to lose even the most stubborn of fat.

Exercise must also have variety. Many people do not

136

exercise because they find it boring, but that is not the fault of the exercise. It may never be the most exciting activity in your life but it can at least be bearable. The boredom most of us suffer, for the most part, will be eliminated if we change exercises periodically. We will still have to contend with our lazy attitude toward physical activity in our nonphysical world, but with periodic exercise changes at least we won't fall asleep while we're exercising.

I find that I get my best results when I shift exercise every four to six weeks. Though I progressively make an exercise harder, my mind and body still need a change. The mind goes stale when it is confronted with excessive repetition. Professional golfers, for instance, complain that a layoff becomes necessary because they are going stale. Their bodies don't get overworked but their minds need rest.

Good results from exercises are linked very closely with the amount of enthusiasm you can generate for the activity. Enthusiasm can be generated if you use variety in your exercise program.

I once worked in a health spa where many of the members had pursued the same exercise programs for over a year. Because they were bored they had not achieved any results for quite some time. I put them on new routines. Quickly attitudes changed and all, without exception, realized significant results—weight loss, endurance improvement, corrected posture or added strength. They gained notable results because they learned how to do the exercise correctly and attack their muscles through different movements.

There are so many exercises available for every part of the body that you cannot possibly run out of them. Not ever. For instance, suppose your physical problem is heavy hips. I can think of at least 100 different exercises specifically for the hips. If you selected three and worked on them for six weeks, you would definitely note some change in your hips. However, continue these same exercises for six months and you would find your results dwindle. There seems to be a law of diminishing returns with regards to benefits from a workout routine. The longer you stay on a program, the less results you receive. I don't mean, however, that you should change programs every two or three weeks. It usually takes at least two weeks to get used to the movements and for any progression to occur through more weight, more reps, more sets, or less rest time between sets. As a rule, change programs every four to six weeks.

Depending on the individual, a time will come when you don't feel like working out. It is then time to change your program. Although it will not always be possible, you should be a little anxious to get into the exercise period. Whether you are eager to get into it or get over it, your best workouts will often occur when you feel least like exercising. Many times I have dreaded the workout only to find when I forced myself to the gym or garage that, since I had to concentrate a little harder than normal because my heart wasn't in it, my muscle concentration was much better.

Because of Greg's work schedule, the only time he could exercise effectively was at 4:30 A.M. He really hates getting up that early in the morning, but he knows how important a regular exercise program is. Since he works out with me I know how many times he wishes he had stayed in bed, but, with much encouragement he keeps at it.

Greg has shared with me on several occasions that some of his best workouts were when he felt least like exercising. He said he experienced a "super workout" when he had to concentrate hard. He concentrated so that he could complete his exercise program and get back to his house. The concentration produced more effective exercise.

I call the boredom that results from an excessively prolonged exercise program, *exercise fatigue.* Your body has progressed as far as it can on the present exercises and it becomes fatigued. At some time in the future, when another change in exercise routine is necessary, this program will once again produce results. Your exercise program must have enough variety to keep your mind from being bored and your body from losing results.

All effective exercise will involve some sort of pain. Not the kind of pain you experience when you break a leg or cut a finger, but nevertheless a real muscular pain. You are exercising muscles that are not in proper condition. The pain in your muscles is communicating that you are exercising correctly and vigorously enough to improve the condition of these muscles. In the beginning you will be a little sore, but as your condition improves, this initial soreness will decrease. However, if you are concentrating on your program, if you are doing the exercises correctly, if you are making the exercises progressively harder, and if you are changing routines regularly, you will *always* feel a little tightness and discomfort in the muscles you are exercising.

When extra demands are placed on blood vessels, such as harder exercising, they expand so that more blood can be fed into the active area. When the exercise stops, the vessels contract to normal size. The tightness and discomfort you feel are the symptoms of this expansion and contraction.

Don't be misled by high-powered salesman, eloquent intelligentsia and uniformed professionals who insist that exercise need not be strenuous or painful. If you want to burn off fatty tissue, firm flabby muscles, and feel fit, you cannot merely go through the motions of exercise. You have to exercise hard enough to feel a tightness or soreness in your muscles to get results. You do not have to be a masochist, but *when your muscles begin to hurt, that is when you should exercise as hard as possible. Results begin when you want to stop.* Don't let muscle pain signal the end of your exercise. Rather, let it be a signpost for a harder, more vigorous workout.

chapter eleven
How Do I Begin?

Since we are communicating by print and not face to face, I would not attempt to prescribe a truly personalized exercise routine for you. I have no idea of your background or your aspirations for your body. We can, however, introduce a basic program from which everyone will benefit. Because it is a beginning, we will concentrate exclusively upon the problem areas that are common to most of us.

Our fat problems seem to collect in the middle of our bodies—waist, sides, abdomen, lower back, upper thighs, hips, and buttocks. These are areas that can be improved on all of us. It is sad indeed, therefore, to see a man or woman without a flat, muscular midsection.

The correct diet, with the raw vegetable salad at night, will help to eliminate lower abdominal bloat, but these middle body muscles must be exercised to become strong, firm and free of fat.

Observe the following routine for six weeks to eight weeks. Perform the exercises first thing in the morning Monday through Saturday. After each workout you will have a healthy appetite for a heavy breakfast. The only equipment you will need is a clock with a second hand. Here we go.

Your beginning routine consists of five exercises which you complete without any rest between exercises. As soon as you finish one exercise, proceed right into the next. Do as many as you can of each exercise. Start with five minutes for the whole exercise program, then add one minute a week. In six weeks you will be exercising ten minutes nonstop. This may not sound like a very long time but you will find it is more than enough. Like most things in life, it is not quantity but quality that counts. Concentrate totally on what you are doing and get the most out of the exercise. After six weeks you are ready for a change.

Lower Back

A popular *non-food* drink advertises that their product is designed for the NOW generation. Judging by the number of bottles and cans we buy of this *non-food*, they must be right. We are also a BACK generation—bad back, that is. Most of us at some time or another have suffered from back pain and usually the problem lies in the lower back, which seems to be the weak link in our body. We have no one but ourselves to blame, for if we do not regularly exercise a muscle, it will get weak and thus be incapable of performing normal duties, much less enduring any strenuous demands. The sore lower back of the weekend athlete is proof positive that we neglect this important part of our bodies.

The lower back is one of our two most critical areas. (The other one is our knees.) *Anything* we do affects the lower back. If something is wrong with it, all activities become a little harder and a bit more painful.

Most people would be surprised to discover that much of that large waist measurement comes from the fat deposited on either side of the spinal column. Exercising the lower back will lower the waist measurement as well as help to tighten the front of the body. These muscles, front and back, work together. You will not find someone with a muscular midsection and a fat back or vice-versa. But the effects on the lower back from abdominal exercise are not enough to guarantee a strong lower back. You need exercise *directly and specifically* for this muscle group.

Daily our lower backs are punished. We bend over desks, sit behind typewriters, stay cooped up in offices and our backs get little chance for exercise. The most damaging aspect of white collar work concerns lack of mobility. Your lower back stays in the same basic position most of the day, experiencing little stretching or contracting of muscles. When muscles are frozen, so to speak, in the same position, they shorten in their total range of movement. This is true *muscle boundness.* Muscles need to be extended and contracted through their natural, total range of movement to maintain good muscle tone and muscle efficiency.

The average American has a difficult time touching his toes. Apart from physical abnormalities, this is because his lower back has not been used for stretching movements. Fortunately, however, this condition can be corrected at any age. I once worked with three men, all over 70 years of age. They had never been able to

When doing stiff-legged toe touchers
be sure to keep the legs perfectly
straight through the whole movement.

Diagram A

touch their toes with their legs straight. In three weeks they were touching their palms on the floor. Their tight, short muscles were now flexible.

In our beginning routine we will use what I consider the best lower back exercise: stiff-legged toe touchers. The movement is simple and very effective. Diagram A illustrates the exercise better than I could explain it. Remember, your legs should stay perfectly straight through the whole movement. Bend over as far as you can, and pull in your stomach as much as you possibly can when you return to the upright position.

Do as many as you can. Shoot for 10 to 20. Then you will be ready for the next part of the body.

Obliques

The obliques or, as they are often called, "love handles." account for another problem. The sides of the waist receive very little exercise.

Besides being unattractive, heavy obliques can cause certain back problems. Heavy weight on either side of the spinal column may compress the spine or twist it, forcing it to move from its normal position. The back has enough trouble fighting bad posture habits without fat pushing it from side to side.

The best exercise for the obliques, which has many varieties, is the side bend. Diagram B explains the exercise. Please remember to hold your stomach in, lift your lung cage, and concentrate on s-t-r-e-t-c-h-i-n-g. S-t-r-e-t-c-h-i-n-g the muscle.

Do as many as you can, perhaps 10 to 20, and then you will be ready for the next part of the body.

Abdominals

The front or the abdominal area comprises the part of the waist we seem to notice first. Since our stomachs

When doing side bends hold your stomach in,
lift your lung cage and concentrate on
s-t-r-e-t-c-h-i-n-g the muscle.

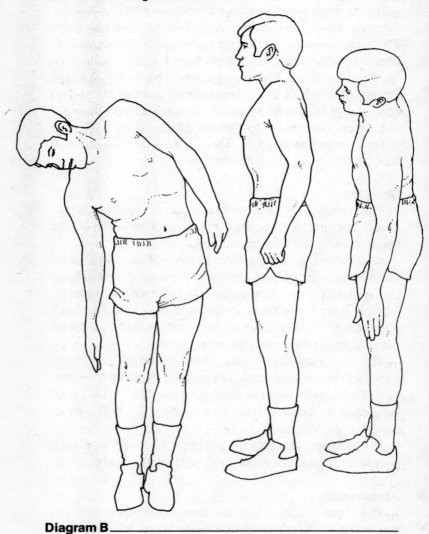

Diagram B

and digestive systems are located here, surplus and poorly digested food is stored here first, causing the pot belly. Muscles are covered by fat because we feed them too much and exercise them too little.

Sitting behind a desk only makes the situation worse. It is really quite hard to hold your stomach up as gravity pulls it down. Slouching forward adds to the problem. The abdominal area is just a very hard area to keep muscular. While you are going through your daily chores, you can help firm this trouble spot by trying to touch your "belly button to your backbone." It takes a conscious effort at first, but after a bit you acquire the habit of "holding yourself in."

Because abdominal muscles cover and therefore protect delicate organs responsible for digestion, assimilation and excretion, your whole body will benefit from strong abdominal muscles. Abdominal exercise will keep these organs operating at top efficiency.

Exercise dilates blood vessels for better circulation, and this circulation helps the body to secrete sufficient digestive juices to do the tasks required. You will never have a problem with irregularity if you undertake a program of regular, progressive exercise that involves some abdominal activity. This is extremely important when you consider the monumental job your large intestinal tract and colon must perform in the elimination of body wastes. Strong muscles in the stomach area—not merely good food, although good food is mandatory for total health—aid in moving waste and digestion by-products from the digestion area to elimination zones. As I said earlier, that little or big pot or pooch may be uneliminated waste. *Make muscles strong and push wastes out.*

For your abdominal exercise, lie flat on your back on the floor. Put your hands under your buttocks. Lift your chest as high as possible and flatten your stomach as

Diagram C

When doing the abdominal exercise,
lie flat on your back, put your hands under
your buttocks, lift your chest as high as possible
and flatten your stomach as hard as you can.

Next, without lifting buttocks from floor,
bend your legs and pull your knees
up into your abdominal area.

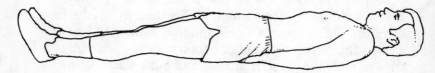

Return legs to floor and repeat.

hard as you can. Your legs should be straight and touching the floor. Without lifting your buttocks off the floor, bend your legs and pull your knees up as high as you can into your abdominal area. Then let them down to the floor again. As soon as your feet touch the floor, do another "knee chest." This exercise is extremely effective for those with minor or chronic back problems. Look at diagram C.

Do as many as you can, usually 10 to 20, and then you will be ready for the next part of the body.

The Big Three

In light of today's revealing fashions, male or female cannot afford the luxury of heaviness in the *big three*— hips, thighs, and buttocks. Next to the midsection, this has to be the area of our greatest concern. A "heavy-hipped mama" may occasion clever-sounding musical lyrics, but few women would agree that this is a condition they are eagerly awaiting. Executives suffer in the big three areas too. As one climbs the proverbial ladder of success and reaps the financial benefits, he also reaps the "executive spread"—a heavy, soft, flabby rear end. All that sitting does not produce firm muscles.

Besides being unattractive, this fat can, and often does, play an important part in later deterioration of the hips. Exercise strengthens not only muscles but also bones and joints. Without sufficient exercise, joints do not get the lubrication or the nutrients necessary to maintain their health and good bone density. Like all other tissue, bones undergo constant building and tearing down. When you exercise your thighs you also work the hips. They all work together.

Knees

Your knees, the hinges of activity, are the second

weakest part of your body (your back is the weakest). If you do not oil a door hinge regularly, it begins to squeak and eventually wears down the metal in the hinge and freezes shut. Exercise is the oil for the knees. Regular and progressive exercise sends greater supplies of blood containing certain "oiling nutrients" to this area. Creaking in the knees is a signal that joints are not receiving enough activity.

Ligaments and tendons, like muscles, get stronger with use. In our contemporary age, supportive tissues are abused constantly. Athletic people especially are guilty of performing certain activities that the body can do, but that are not best for the body. Twisting and changing directions as in football or basketball, running or stopping quickly as in tennis, putting all the weight on the inside weak part of the knees as in some gymnastics movements or golf, jogging on hard surfaces like asphalt or concrete all present serious problems for ligaments and tendons. Unless some corrective and preventive exercise is employed, injuries are inevitable.

Ligaments stretch like rubber bands. Extend a rubber band beyond its range of movement and it will snap. A torn ligament is repaired only by surgery, but once it is repaired, it can never be "unstretched." You will always have a little extra play. When you run and then stop, an injured and repaired knee will not stop as quickly as a non-injured knee. Regular and progressive exercise, therefore, will help offset many of the potential dangers you are likely to experience during certain strenuous activities and may save you the pain and expense of a knee operation.

The athletic person is not the only one to suffer knee problems. Persons who lack sufficient activity also have problems: weak ligaments, tight muscles, poor flexibility and a short range of movement. These physical limitations are the results, not the causes, of knee problems. No matter what body structure you were born with, you have potential for full range in your knees as well as in all your limbs.

The best exercise for your knees, hips and buttocks is the full squat. Yes, I said the *full squat*. Half movements make for shortened muscles. Full squats or deep knee bends provide the very best exercise because the movement is a natural movement for your legs. There is no danger whatsoever in squats as long as you do them correctly. Look carefully at diagram D.

There are several points to remember when doing squats.

Keep your knees pointing out. Don't let your knees buckle in. The inside part of the knee is the weak part, where many injuries occur. Turn your toes and knees out. This places a significant amount of strain on the inside part of the thighs where much fat lies.

Go all the way down. Don't do half squats or less. You want a full range of movement so that muscles, ligaments and tendons are stretched to their full length. Your squat should end at the position where your upper legs touch your lower legs. This is a full squat. Such a movement will guarantee that no part of your thigh escapes the exercise.

Keep your back straight. When you come to the bottom of your squat, thighs and calves should lightly touch; then return to an erect position. If you are long-legged, you may want to put a block of wood or a book under your heels. This will enable you to stay more erect. Bouncing at the bottom of your squat may produce a tearing of those ligaments supporting and connecting your knees. This radical relaxing and tightening of the ligaments precipitates many knee injuries. The movement must be smooth and steady with very little

Correct

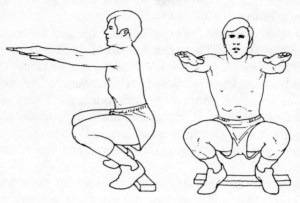

To do the full squat correctly, keep back
straight and knees pointing out. Do *not* bounce
as you come to the bottom of the movement.

Incorrect

When doing the full squat incorrectly the
back is bent and the knees are pointed in.

bounce at the bottom. In this manner the muscles are being exercised with no ill effect on the connective tissue.

Now do as many as you can, 10 to 20, and then you will be ready for the last exercise.

The last exercise in our beginning program involves a brief run around the house. Just let your arms dangle by your sides and loosely jog around the house. See diagram E.

When running,
let arms dangle loosely at sides,
take 20 to 30 running steps per
foot at first, increase number
as you gain conditioning.

Diagram E

You are not trying to break any speed records; just keep your body moving. Start with 20 to 30 running steps per foot and then, without stopping, go back and resume the whole set of exercises. Do as many of these exercise cycles (one exercise cycle would be all five exercises) as you can in five minutes, and *do not stop during the entire five minutes*. Be a perpetual motion machine for five minutes, but do the exercises in this order:

- Stiff Legged Toe Touches
- Side Bends
- Knee Chest
- Squats
- Run

To keep making it progressive, add repetitions per each movement and increase the exercise period by one minute per week until you reach 10 minutes nonstop. This will be in six weeks.

chapter twelve
It Works; Try It

I told you in the beginning that the material in this book would be unlike anything you have read before but at the same time would make good sense to you. The principles are simple and can be incorporated into any life-style if— and only if—you want to lose that extra weight and keep it off *permanently*. You do not need expensive medical assistance, complicated gimmicks or special wonder systems. YOU are really the only expensive equipment you will need. The proof is right around the scales. It works; try it.

Let's review a few important points.

1. *Eat food, not non-food.* The supermarket merchandises many items not fit to enter your body. If the product has a chemical name or contains those *non-*

foods we have discussed, *read it but don't eat it.* Eat only *food,* because only food feeds the body.

2. *Cultivate a healthy eating pattern.* You have been raised with a certain kind of eating pattern. Unfortunately, it is the wrong kind of eating pattern. You can, however, radically reverse this procedure by eating your big meal in the morning, a medium-sized meal at midday, and a light meal at night. Protein should be consumed at the two daytime meals, roughage in the form of raw vegetables and sometimes raw fruit at night. In this way the body gets a good cleansing every night and is ready for a big meal in the morning when your activity begins. You will therefore be burning up the food you are eating rather than storing it as fat. Your digestion will improve, your sleep will be more restful, and your excretory organs will better eliminate harmful poisons which will, in effect, help to slow down the aging process.

3. *When you are physically inactive, your mind dictates what your body wants. When you are physically active, your body dictates what your body wants.* If we are to keep our desires for food on a healthy plane, we need to be active enough to allow our bodies to control what we need to eat to sustain us. Out of boredom and anxiety our minds sometimes push us to crave things that are not good for us. A physically active person has a much smaller desire for these bandages for emotional stress because his physical activity is giving him an avenue for expression. When this expression is not forthcoming, food will often be the drug we use to make the bleak bright and the boredom bearable. Eat to live; don't live to eat.

4. *Exercise must be added to the recipe for good health.* Regardless of what anyone tells you, exercise is the most important element for good health. You can

even compensate for many bad habits with exercise. This is not to suggest that you can maintain your old bad habits, for bad habits should be replaced like worn-out shoes. They are no longer of any use. Exercise is the X-factor that is missing from most health programs. Include it in your health program—regular, specific, hard, correct, progressive and varied. All of these elements are necessary to produce the results that make your investment of time worthwhile.

5. *Muscle exhaustion vs. oxygen exhaustion.* Very few of us have exercised to the point where our muscles are totally exhausted. We usually run out of oxygen long before we are able to push our muscles to the point where they can no longer function. When we exercise our muscles to the point of muscle exhaustion, we get the most work out of those muscles being used. We will get results much quicker. It is not quantity but quality. When you approach total muscle exhaustion, you will unfortunately experience some discomfort, but don't let this stop you. While exercising your muscles to the point of exhaustion, you are also improving your cardiovascular system and your ability to more effectively use the oxygen in your system. This kind of physical training will definitely improve your proficiency in any activity and, in addition, attack specific muscles that need your careful attention.

6. *Let your drive be your guide.* Regardless of how long you have endured your present physical condition, you can change it. *You are not stuck with you.* Using the principles we have discussed in this book, you will learn that *imagination* (picturing what you want to look like) plus *concentration* (putting in the time and drive to work for this goal) equals *success* (the kind of body you really want).

If you want to be *Fit and Free*—free from overweight,

157

free from a rundown condition, free from aches and pains, free from the *non-food* that glitters before us in the marketplace, free from excuses about why we cannot do the things we used to be able to do, free from the humdrum existence that so many of us experience because of our unhealthy habits—follow the precepts in this book and you will see things happen that you never thought possible. The results are yours if you have the *need* to be *Fit and Free*.

bibliography

Cheraskin, E., et al. *Diet and Disease.* Emmaus, Penn.: Rodale Press, Inc., 1968.

Clark, Linda. *Stay Young Longer.* New York: Pyramid Publications, 1968.

Hutchins, Kenneth C. *Heart Disease and High Blood Pressure.* New York: Arc Books, Inc., 1964.

LaLanne, Jack. *The Jack LaLanne Way to Vibrant Good Health.* Englewood Cliffs, N.J.: Prentice-Hall, 1960.

J.I. Rodale, *Encyclopedia of Common Diseases.* Emmaus, Penn.: Rodale Press, Inc., 1971.

____*Health Builders*, 1957.

____*Health Seekers*, 1971.

____*Our Poisoned Earth and Sky*, 1964.

Tilden, John H. *Toxemia: The Basic Causes of Disease.* Chicago: Natural Hygiene Press, 1974.

Bibliography